The
WIMBLEDON
FINAL THAT
NEVER WAS...

...And Other Tennis Tales from a Bygone Era

BY SIDNEY WOOD
with DAVID WOOD

The
WIMBLEDON FINAL THAT NEVER WAS...

...And Other Tennis Tales from a Bygone Era

BY SIDNEY WOOD
with DAVID WOOD

NEW CHAPTER PRESS

The Wimbledon Final That Never Was is published by New Chapter Press (www.NewChapterMedia.com) and distributed by the Independent Publishers Group (www.IPGBook.com).
@ David Wood
The book was designed by Kirsten Navin.

New Chapter Press would like to thank Alan Little and Audrey Snell of the Wimbledon Library, Welsh sports writer Leigh Sanders, Greg Sharko with the ATP World Tour, Manfred Wenas with TennisGrandstand.com, Joanie Angler, the International Tennis Hall of Fame, Kirsten Navin, Bill Mountford, Irene Tan, Ewing Walker, Spencer Ain, Christine Schott and Misha Suominen.

A major thank you goes out to Joe Stahl, whose passion for tennis and this book is greatly appreciated. Your tireless editing and feedback greatly improved this project.

Photos are courtesy of David Wood and the archives and estate of Sidney Wood, except for photos of Gertrude Lawrence, Rene Lacoste, Errol Flynn, Charlie Chaplin, Fay Wray, Groucho Marx, Grace Kelly, Althea Gibson, Bobby Fischer, The Shah of Iran, Henri Cochet and Jean Borotra, which are courtesy of WikiCommons. The ATP logo is courtesy of the ATP World Tour.

ISBN – 978-0942257847
Printed in Canada.

For Sidney Wood III, whose precious life ended at 21.

> *"...The bloom is vanished from my life.*
> *For O! he stood beside me, like my youth,*
> *Transformed for me the real to the dream,*
> *Clothing the palpable and familiar*
> *With golden exhalations of the dawn.*
> *Whatever fortunes waits my toil,*
> *The beautiful is vanished – and returns not."*
> -   *Samuel Taylor Coleridge*
> -   (from Schiller's Wallenstein)

Contents

Introduction

GROWING UP AS A CHILD OF A WIMBLEDON CHAMPION, bedtime was different than that of the average family. While most children were being read bedtime stories about Goldilocks, the Three Little Pigs or other such perfunctory fairy tale fare to lull them to sleep, we were being treated to the likes of Bill Tilden, Don Budge and other titans of tennis from the first part of the 20th century. We came to call them "Nighttime Tilden Stories" – no matter who was the subject.

My father had the distinction of being the youngest man to win the Wimbledon title when he won in 1931 at age 19— thus being recognized as Wimbledon's youngest men's champion for over half a century until Boris Becker swatted that record out of the stadium and into eternity by winning back to back championships in 1985 and 1986 at ages 17 and 18. He still, however, has the dubious distinction of being the only ever Wimbledon winner without having played a final. This anomaly in tennis history resulted in him being awarded "The Wimbledon Final That Never Was" in a walk-over. His best pal, roommate and U.S. Davis Cup teammate Frank Shields, the grandfather of actress and model Brooke Shields, defaulted the final due to a knee injury.

Of course, we didn't have the appreciation in those early days of the magnitude of Pop's accomplishments. Having grown up with it and lacking the perspective of those who had not, we looked upon him as pretty average and even fallible as fathers go. For this reason, those bedtime stories, while great fun at the time, were not set to lasting memory. It was fortunate then that only a few years later, at the suggestion of one of his many delighted listeners, my father began putting to paper the many stories and anecdotes from his extraordinary life with which he had regaled many for decades prior. His intention became to turn all of these accounts into a book called "Aged In Wood." It would be an autobiography of his life in and out of tennis, from his birth and subsequent inauspicious years of serious early childhood illness from which he was not expected to recover, to his triumphs in tennis and business and the many fantastic adventures along the way with friends of note from various walks of life. This book is unique in that you get a perspective, particularly about the game itself, as told by one who started as a protégé of Tilden and had played, or watched play and studied and known personally every player since, all the way up to Roger Federer. There was simply no one else on the planet who could speak with his authority and first-hand knowledge of the game.

I started reading these stories in the late 1970s and, not being a person who was much into reading at all at that time, found myself riveted, not only by the many amazing adventures of which I had never been aware, but also by his witty, breezy writing style that just carried me from page to page. So devoted was he to the writing of this book that he never got around to finishing it. He just couldn't bring himself to stop writing it, even as projected publishing dates came and went. Perhaps he didn't want to let go of the past where he had youth, success, fans and a legion of wonderful and influential friends, virtually all of whom he outlived. Reliving the past through his remembrances gave him joy and vigor, a reason to rise every morning to spend time with the cast of characters that gave him so much joy, and sometimes heartache, throughout his long and productive life. It wasn't until after his passing in January of 2009 at the age of 97, that I was able to retrieve his writings and many files and made the decision to pick up the mantel and finally get this wonderful manuscript in shape for publishing for all to enjoy. As you will see in the following pages, I have interjected some narration throughout the volume to fill in some gaps in my father's writings or to provide proper context.

It is my pleasure to finally make this book available to everyone who loves tennis and its colorful past. It is an invaluable and unique first-hand perspective for tennis fans and students of tennis history from one who lived, and contributed to, that history.

David Wood
2011

Sidney Wood

CHAPTER ONE

Who Am I?

PEOPLE TEND TO REMEMBER MY TENNIS NAME (IF AT all!), not as one of the top three or four American players of my time, but for the uniqueness of being Wimbledon's only winner by default. Even so, I was its youngest men's singles champion at the age of 19 for over 50 years and its youngest male competitor at the age of only 15.

I had never given much thought to remedying this impression until I started digging up a bunch of old records that *Tennis* magazine had requested for a story. I had retained draw sheets of most major tournaments from time immemorial, and when I fished out those of our U.S. Nationals, now the US Open, and saw myself seeded four years at No. 3, twice at No. 4, and once each at No. 5 and No. 6, over an eight-year span. I literally wondered for a moment whether some kind of crazy misprint had occurred. When I then got curious about my international record against the world's top 10, I was again startled and admittedly aglow at finding my one-on-one numbers were a lot more favorable than I'd realized. The only discovery that might top this would be something like a missing birth certificate materializing with a decade-later-than presumed nativity date.

In our day, to be chosen as one of your country's two

Davis Cup singles players was every player's ultimate hope. As a married, depression-years' breadwinner from the time I was 21, paying the rent came before putting trophies on the shelf. Most all of my top-ranked U.S. opponents were holding down tennis-related jobs, permitting practice and tournament play for a good part of the year, but even as a full-time working stiff (though my own boss since 22), I did manage to steal away four times to Wimbledon or on Davis Cup team junkets, but never got within half a globe of Australia.

Most years, I would head east for our late August National Championships from my California gold and sulfur diggings, barely ahead of the first day of the tournament, figuring to adjust to the grass during the first round or two. But let me tell you, more than once I got bounced before I knew where I was. The clanking, metal-body 14-passenger Ford tri-motor planes, replete with sick bags, and ammonia capsules, rarely made it in even twice the 29 hours advertised, usually with risky Rocky-Mountain weather sleepovers on wooden benches at tiny airports. No alibis, only reciting one of the reasons I thought of myself as an underdog against my more frequently competing peers -- though I now may just consider re-writing my epitaph! Striving to maintain whatever tennis eminence one managed to attain in those no-pay-for-play years can't sound too glamorous, but I wouldn't trade a single season's memory for whatever goes for achievement and camaraderie today.

CHAPTER TWO

Early Years

I WAS BORN ON NOVEMBER 1, 1911 IN A PLACE CALLED Black Rock, Connecticut, near Bridgeport. I don't remember much about the years before moving to California, but I was told that I spent four years on my back. I was a very sick young man with a variety of childhood diseases that in today's world of medicine is not serious. But back in the days when I was an infant, they were often fatal.

My father owned a mine out in Arizona which called for my early family life to be spent out West. As a youngster, I started to play tennis because I couldn't play other sports competitively. My mother took me out to play. I remember the first court I ever played on was at the mining camp made of crushed stone. I don't know if that influenced me to develop a short swing but that was the only way you could hit the ball.

My first racquet that I used to practice against the house wall, or I should say the windows (and I broke one occasionally), was one that my uncle Watson Washburn left in the closet when he went to Australia to play on the U.S. Davis Cup team with Bill Tilden. (Uncle "Watty" subsequently became captain of the U.S. Davis Cup team.) His racquet was sitting there in the closet and I picked it out. That heralded my departure from being a budding pianist (my mother was

3

teaching me music at that time). I was never sure if she was totally happy with the change, but I was.

My tennis was played almost all in California until I was about 13. The first time I saw my uncle Watty, I was fifteen and about to play in the National Junior Championships. My first real competition was in California and one of the most thrilling prizes I won was a turkey, which probably described the way I played in those days, but, this was a handicapped

Wood as a child champion

mixed doubles tournament in Golden Gate Park in San Francisco, and I lived in Berkeley. I won the prize to everyone's dismay because I was literally as high as the net. I was an infant in size. I really didn't grow into my final huge stature of 5' 9 3/4 until I seemed to get out of all these physical problems.

I brought the turkey home by ferry, which was then the means of transport between San Francisco and Berkeley, as the Golden Gate Bridge, Bay Bridge or even Alcatraz had not been built yet! I remember my mother completely broke up. She already had a turkey cooked, but nobody could believe that I was going to bring home the bacon, if you'll forgive the mixed metaphor, or simile. That was a big thrill because it was really an upset that I should win anything at that size. It was a grown-up mixed doubles tournament and I was the only "infant" in it.

I literally lived in tennis shoes at that time. This is what happens when you have had health problems. You're just dying to excel at something to bring you out of the rut that you have been in. To give you a little philosophy, Glen Cunningham, who was the greatest miler for many years, and whom I sold bonds with on a tour once, had his legs severely burned. He was told he would never walk again. He, of course, went on to become the world's greatest miler. There are repeats of stories like this down the line with so many people who are handicapped who overcome their disabilities and become great achievers. Now with so many luxuries – it's hard to get children to do what we found easy to do.

Schoolwork was very sporadic. I never learned multiplication tables, how to write correctly and other things that children ordinarily learn. Going up to the blackboard was always an embarrassment and a struggle. I would finally get sick with worry that I would stay out of school and have to have a tutor, which taught me nothing because you can always con a tutor. In summary, I really learned nothing in school.

I finally went to school in New York one winter, when I was 14. I suffered so much that I lost 14 pounds in the space of three months and was immediately rushed to Arizona because I developed some problems with my lungs.

For four months, I rested and played checkers with some older people in Memorial Park in Tucson. I always wondered

Wood won the Arizona State Men's Tennis Championships at age 14

why these people would always have colds and be coughing a lot (nobody told me they were there because of tuberculosis).

I learned to play checkers with a passion, but continued to keep up with my tennis. I went off to Phoenix to play in the Arizona State Men's Tennis Championship at the age of 14 and weighing well under 90 pounds. To some surprise, I won the title, beating in the final a young guy who was very frightened because all of my friends from my checkers games came over to watch me play. And I got a headline in the Tucson paper about four inches high "Tucson Boy Genius Returns."

The win got me an invitation to play in the French Championships and Wimbledon. In Paris, I won my first round match 0-6, 8-6, 2-6, 6-3, 6-4 over Paul Barrelet de Ricou of France, but I lost in the second round to Jack Condon of South Africa 6-3, 6-1, 6-4.

From there, I played my first Wimbledon. I met the great Frenchman Rene Lacoste, the No. 1 seed, in the first round. (They probably wanted to get this over-precocious American out of the tournament.) One of my nicest memories is that I have a picture of the scoreboard and it shows me leading 3-1 in the second set, either because of his kindness, or carelessness. I lost the match 6-1, 6-3, 6-1 but entered the record books as the youngest man to ever compete at The Championships at age 15 years, 231 days.

The next year, at the age of 16, I returned to Wimbledon and got to the third round where I lost to Pierre Henri Landry of France in four sets. The next day, Landry lost to Bill Tilden in five sets.

Upon arrival back in the States, the first tournament was Seabright, N.J. I played Fritz Merker, who had just beaten Tilden the week before at the Westchester Biltmore Eastern

Wood, 15, played René Lacoste in the first round at Wimbledon in 1927

Grass Court Championships. Weighing less than 100 pounds, I beat Fritz by serving aces (I had a whippy serve). This started a pretty good run of play that year. Even at 16, people didn't take me lightly.

Our family went to California every winter, but there was no one to play with except Ellsworth Vines, the powerful American player who would go on to win Wimbledon once and the U.S. Championship twice. I had a car and I'd go to the Los Angeles Tennis Club and play. Elly and I played tennis but eventually I took up golf and Elly played with me.

Here we were, two tennis players playing golf every chance we got! He subsequently became a golf pro after his tennis career and ranked in the top ten after a couple of years on the tour. I got sufficiently adept at golf, so when they had the Pasadena Open tournament that year, I decided to play even though I'd never broken 80 before. When I hit the ball in the sand trap, I'd putt the ball out - no one ever taught me any differently. But I played and broke 80 in the open tournament and was somewhere in the first 18 scorers on the first day. This was with such standout golf legends as Walter Hagen and Horton Smith in the field. The next day, I asked my friends to come out and watch and, at the end of about 15 holes, I was at 104. I went in every bunker and was a nervous wreck. I went back and got my racquet out of mothballs and started playing tennis again.

I then entered the Pacific Southwest tournament in Los Angeles and I had one day of practice after the golf tournament. Bunny Austin, Henri Cochet and Keith Gledhill were the top players in the field. I wasn't even seeded, but I beat Keith in the first round to everyone's horror because he was the Southern California hope at the time and I had just come off the golf course. I then beat Johnny Van Ryn and Bunny Austin. Cochet got me in the semifinals, but the results showed me that I had something to offer to tennis, so I started playing again.

That fall, I went consistently to school, attending the Rox-

Frank Shields at Forest Hills

bury School in Cheshire, Connecticut, a preparatory school. I was supposed to go to Harvard since my four uncles went there, but I was presumed to be uneducated (which I was with my horrible tutoring). The main reason I went to Roxbury was because Frank Shields was there. Frank and I would not only turn into lifelong friends, but we would be forever linked in tennis history for the matches (and non-matches) we played against each other in addition to being Davis Cup teammates, doubles partners, business partners and being inducted together into the International Tennis Hall of Fame in 1964. Although by the end of the century Frank would be better known as the grandfather of model/actress Brooke Shields, he was a legend of a man in his time.

Frank and I went from Roxbury to the summer grass court circuit. This was 1930 and it was among my most exciting years of competitive tennis as I was breaking through in a sport that had been part of my whole life. I was playing with the likes of people that included some of the top international players of the era. I played first at the Longwood Bowl tournament at Longwood Cricket Club in Boston and reached the final before losing 6-4, 6-3, 6-2 to Clifford Sutter, then the collegiate singles champion from Tulane. It was a match I felt I was able to have taken control of, but I was not really match tough at that point in the summer. But I won the doubles with a wonderful friend, Harold Blauer, who was not the greatest singles player, maybe not the greatest doubles player either, but he was for me. He looked so crazy going up to net that sometimes I'd turn around when he was serving to take a look and I'd practically break apart laughing at him. He'd also do whatever I said (in doubles it's good to have one director) and he never missed a forehand in the right court. He never failed to put it down to the opponents' feet and never failed to lob on his backhand. With Harold not being a player of recognized caliber, this was very exciting for me.

After taking a week off, I entered Seabright but was not seeded there with a wealth of good players in the draw. Again, Vines drew all the press notices and got to the final, this time beating Frank in the semis. I almost laughed my way into the final because I was thrilled with the way I was hitting the ball. I beat Sutter in the semis (the last set being a love set), but was practically ignored in the press because Vines had already won the tournament in everybody's eyes. The night before the final, I remember telling Vinnie Richards that I had a formula for beating Vines.

This match was kind of a key point in my career. It confirmed my belief that you could invent an idea and, even if it was faulty in its premise, it was still good to stick with it. If you come into a match with a purpose or idea of how you're going to play a match (even if it's wrong) it stabilizes your psyche and your nervous system. It gives you a direction and purpose and a concentration on one particular thing which seems to take care of all the other problems. Almost all players in the top 20 in the world play with some basic level of execution. It's the guys who dream a little idea up or who know when to gamble on the right point who take things to a higher level.

So I told Vinnie, who believed in my game, that I thought I detected in Vines' game a tendency to overstretch (extend) his arm and that he loved to hit balls that came at him with a lot of pace. He used to hit Frank's bludgeoning first serve back as if he was catching it and throwing it back. So I said, "I'm going to hit outside slice serves and if he starts to move over,

Roxbury School pals Wood and Shields

I'm going to slice it into his backhand the same way. I'm not going to hit a hard serve in the beginning and I believe he'll float a lot of these and hit the fence with some of them." I told Allison Danzig, the tennis reporter from *The New York Times,* the same thing.

When you're that age, you are blooming with confidence, but let's just say there may be a little skepticism on the part of your listeners when you recite a crazy program like this. But we went out and the first four games was a feel-out thing and we each held serve twice. Vines was having a terrible time bringing his shots down. He wasn't catching them wrong on his racquet, but he was forced to move the wrong foot forward. In other words, he was forced to take a little skip to get his foot out, and that completely destroyed his ability to pivot. This gave me such confidence and having that singular purpose insulated me from any other problems. I found I was taking his serve as if it were nothing and just putting it back with good control. The minute we got into a rally, I began to spin it. If I got the ball to my backhand on a point that was feasible to do it, I would "violin slice" the ball to his forehand to draw it away. Maybe he just got mesmerized, I don't know, but he was wondering what I was doing and got upset that somebody was doing something different against him.

From 2-2 in the first set, I won the match 6-2, 6-0. I took ten straight games. I completely destroyed his shots, and believe it or not, I was castigated in the press by a couple of writers who had already written their story with Vines winning! I was practically accused of cheating by soft-balling, which I wasn't. The balls were going slowly because they had spin on them. I remember a writer from New York, J.P. Allen, actually was furious with me for these tactics. He said I played like my grandmother (I hope she played that way!).

Flush with success, I then went on to play in the event in Southampton at the Meadow Club, where the draw was made before the seedings could reflect the result of my win at Seabright, so I was not seeded as high as I would have been otherwise. Everyone had just come back from Wimbledon - Tilden, who'd won it, Wilmer Allison, who'd lost to Tilden

Wood is presented the Seabright trophy after beating Ellisworth Vines

in the final after beating Cochet in the semifinals, and George Lott, who'd won the doubles with Van Ryn. I met Lott in the round of 16 in a match I'll never forget because it was the first time I had had an experience with an adrenaline attack.

We were in the third set and George had me 5-1, 40-0 on his serve and I suddenly felt my hair stand up a little bit. I thought I was having a sunstroke, so I went and sat in a linesman's chair and put some ice on myself. All of a sudden, I wanted to cry and burst into tears. I went back and – this sounds untrue but it's absolutely the way it is and it happened to me again several times – I saw the ball as if it were twice as large, with absolute, total clarity. From the second it left George's racquet, it was like a sphere coming over, like a satellite with a little fuzz around it and there was no way I was going to miss it.

George served three serves to my backhand with the intention of coming in -- that's how George played -- and I passed him clean three times with placements. No volleys. I came back and won the match, five times facing match point.

The next day, I played Frank in the semifinals. It was the first time we'd played since the spring at the Roxbury School. Frank, unbelievably, had beaten Tilden the day before and had served don't ask me how many clean aces. But Tilden was just coming back from winning Wimbledon, and was defeated by some ridiculous score like 6-3, 6-1. Frank was just serving ace after ace and completely destroyed Tilden's ego. I later learned from Wimbledon trips and Davis Cup trips that in those days of boat travel, for whatever reason it was, sea legs was a very important factor. Nobody really realized it, but nobody really played their top game the first week after they got back. Frank, however, was playing beautiful tennis, busting every ball he hit.

Frank jumped out to a terrific start against me, winning the first two sets 6-1, 6-1 serving the same way he did against Tilden. I didn't seem to be able to get ahold of the ball at all. I had this built-in respect for Frank, who was gigantic in size (six foot, four inches) and also my good friend. I just couldn't get up that feeling of an intense rivalry and, at the same time, was totally euphoric at having won all these great matches to reach the semifinals. I had never been able to beat Frank at school in practice. He always sort of manhandled me, so I probably had this inferior feeling. Leading two-sets-to-love, Frank had me 5-3 and 30-15 on his serve. Don't ask me how I won the set, but I did. The next set, we got into the same thing and Frank had me 5-3 with two match points. Somehow, I won that set too.

Meantime, we were both getting cramps and falling down on the court. I'd run over and grab Frank's leg and try to pull the cramp out of his leg and he'd do the same for me. In those days, it was gentlemen's tennis. Nobody was going to kill each other and we were buddies, roommates and everything else. I have no idea how, but at the end of the day, I was the last man standing and won the match 1-6, 1-6, 10-8, 7-5, 6-4. Danzig, in *The New York Times*, said that the match was "one of the most dramatic and exhausting that has been witnessed on the turf courts of the Meadow Club in the 47-years' history of the fixture."

Allison was my opponent the next day in the final. Now remember, this is Southampton. I'd won the tournament the week before at Seabright and I'm now just about as callow and immature as you can be and unaccustomed to all the adulation and whatever it was that went with it. People were treating me like a man and I was really still a child. Allison had beaten Frank Hunter. Vines had been upset by Lott before I beat him. Vines, in fact, withdrew after playing one set, claiming fatigue.

Again, I found myself in a hole, only to crawl my way out. In the fifth set, I was down 0-3, 0-40 on my serve, but somehow won that game. I got on another roll and won five of the last six games and won the match 3-6, 6-3, 2-6, 6-2, 6-4 to win the title. Danzig called me a "thin-faced, golden-haired Houdini of the courts" for my three come-from-behind wins and called my efforts "the most impressive winning streak accredited in years to a single player in the course of one tournament."

At the end of that summer, based on his wins in Southampton and at Seabright and his runner-up showing at Longwood, my father was awarded the No. 4 seed at the U.S. Nationals at Forest Hills at the age of 18.

Bill Tilden, who won at Wimbledon earlier in the summer, was accorded with the top seeding, as he was the defending champion and seeking his record-breaking eighth U.S. men's singles title. Wilmer Allison of Texas, the Wimbledon runner-up, was seeded No. 2 and George Lott of Illinois at No. 3. Frank Shields, at the age of 20, was seeded No. 11.

My father had the distinction of "opening" the tournament, playing the first match of the event on the famed horseshoe-shaped stadium, beating Weller Evans in the first round. In the quarterfinals, he avenged his loss to Clifford Sutter in the Longwood final by beating the New Orleans standout 6-4, 6-3, 2-6, 7-5 in the waning late afternoon light.

Shields advanced to a semifinal showing with my dad with a bit more difficulty, coming back from two-sets-to-love-down against Gregory

Mangin of Newark, N.J., 3-6, 6-8, 6-2, 6-1, 6-1.

My father and Shields were the two "young guns" on the scene and their semifinal match was met with much anticipation. Wrote Allison Danzig in The New York Times, *"When Sidney B. Wood, Jr. goes up against Frank Shields today, two of the youngest players ever to gain the penultimate round of the championship and also two of America's most brilliant Davis Cup prospects will throw down the gauntlet to each other."*

Shields was the better man on the day, using his booming serve to perfection and beating my father 6-2, 6-3, 4-6, 6-3 to advance to the U.S. singles final. Their match, however, did not receive much fanfare that day as Johnny Doeg, a 21-year-old left-hander out of Stanford University, staged an upset for the ages beating the 37-year-old Tilden in the other semifinal 10-8, 6-3, 3-6, 12-10, canceling Big Bill's chance to win an eighth U.S. title.

The tournament became, more or less, a changing of the guard or an end of an era event as it marked the final major championship of the Tilden era. Doeg followed up his monumental win over Tilden by beating Shields 10-8, 1-6, 6-4, 16-14 for the championship.

Tilden subsequently announced that he would turn professional, shying away from the amateur lawns of Wimbledon and Forest Hills and setting the table for the new post Tilden era of tennis beginning in 1931. My father and his pal Frank Shields would be among a cast of characters, including other newcomers Doeg, Ellsworth Vines, Jack Crawford of Australia and Fred Perry of Britain as well veterans such as Henri Cochet and Jean Borotra of France, who would seek glory on the tennis courts of the world.

- David Wood

CHAPTER THREE

The Wimbledon Final That Never Was....

THE MOST EXCITING YEAR OF MY LIFE IN TENNIS WAS 1931. I spent that winter with three friends homesteading in Arizona and went to the University of Arizona. I was then called to the colors, to go down to Mexico to represent the United States in Davis Cup play with Frank Shields, Wilmer Allison and Johnny Van Ryn. From there, I went to Canada, and from there over to Wimbledon. We skipped the French Championships and went directly to Wimbledon. From there, we were then going to play Davis Cup against Great Britain in Paris two weeks after Wimbledon in the Inter-zone finals.

Any tournament player knows that in critical matches, where tension can put a deep-freeze on his reflexes, even a momentary distraction can thaw his jitters and normalize his reaction. During the two weeks of match play against the world's best that must be survived to come away with a Wimbledon singles title, I was on such a romantic cloud that there was not even a passing anxiety before or during any of my matches, however much higher each opponent was rated. This was the result of an unlikely friendship that blossomed between your fairly junior tennis hopeful and the universally adored, nonpareil queen of musical comedy, the scintillating Gertrude Lawrence.

Gertrude Lawrence

I played at such a high level at Wimbledon in 1931 because of the inspiration I got having this wonderful creature rooting for me in the gallery, sitting in my player's seat, which was behind a column by the way. She'd lean around this way or that to be able to see me.

We met aboard the *R.M.S. Mautetania*, on which our U.S. Davis Cup team was en route to London. The spell was first cast when Gertie invited me to join her at the Captain's table. I was 19 and Gertie some ten years my senior, but she had the zest and gaiety of a teenager. In London, her rehearsals notwithstanding, we had dinner most nights during the tournament. Each day, the chauffeured Bentley would pick me up at Grosvenor House, usually with Gertie within, but always with Noel Coward, who wasn't doing too badly in show business with a never before or since approached, three simultaneous boffo London hits to celebrate. With all this going on, he still never missed a day at Wimbledon and was perhaps my most uninhibited rooter. The fact that "our" Bentley would invariably make it to the All England Club a good five minutes ahead of the U.S. Davis Cup team's assigned sedate Daimler was not without its pleasures.

I was seeded No. 7 and beat Patrick Hughes of Great Britain in the quarterfinals. I was supposed to play Henri Cochet, the No. 2 seed, in that round, but Nigel Sharpe of Britain had beaten him 6-1, 6-3, 6-2 in a crazy first-round upset.

In the semifinals, I played "the unbeatable" Fred Perry. The night before, our non-playing U.S. Davis Cup Captain Sam Hardy ordained that I must hit the hay early. However, after tossing around until midnight, I called Gertie at the Kit Kat Club, where she had told me she would be late-supping after rehearsal. I said I'd be right over. Frank, my roommate who was scheduled to play his semifinal against the No. 1 seed and two-time champion Jean Borotra the next day, rolled over and regarded me with some wonderment as I got into my rented white tie and tails and headed out (such apparel was then not only *de rigeuer* but prerequisite for entering a respectable night club). Curiously, I met Borotra there at the club, who was scheduled to play Frank, and I said, laughing, "What are you doing here?" He responded with his thick French accent, "What are you doing here Sidney?" My excuse was simply, "I can't sleep."

You shouldn't get the idea that this was normal training, but the fact is I was mad about Gertie, and if you can't sleep anyway, what's the point of tossing and turning. Gertie had her customary coterie of admiring nightlife people around, which often included the then Prince of Wales and his Queen-not-to-be, Wallace Simpson, whose New York apartment had adjoined my mother's and whose later marriage to the abdicated king would rock even Gibraltar. At a late hour, we departed the club and caroled our way through deserted London streets.

I slept like a sloth until noon, had a huge brunch; and Gertie and Noel picked me up for my semifinal against an unsuspecting, earthbound Perry. I felt like a million bucks. About all I remember of the match was that I would keep looking up at my players' section seats, which were then half obstructed by a column (but who cared!?), and there was Gertie, waving a little lace handkerchief, and some 12,000 people craning their necks to see whatever was going on. It was desperately flattering, and there was no thought in my mind of not winning. I tried a number of low percentage, show-off shots, which naturally worked like magic, and the match turned into something of a runaway, as were my previous rounds. I was in another roseate, tension-free Gertie Lawrence realm throughout that euphoric Wimbledon fortnight.

I raced out to a ridiculous lead, something like 4-0, but ended up losing the first set 6-4. I was completely informal. I mean I had no worry about the match because of this vision that I had watching me. It was the semifinals of Wimbledon and I was overjoyed, as far as I was concerned. That's as far as anybody should have to go in tennis, of course I'd still die to win, but again, it was the thrill of just being there. It wasn't vital to me that I win that match. Sounds ridiculous, doesn't it? I was not dying from nervousness or anything else. I won the next three sets very handily 6-2, 6-4, 6-2, in fact I don't even remember it being a difficult match, and there I was – in the final at Wimbledon.

In the other semifinal, Borotra was a guy who if I had to

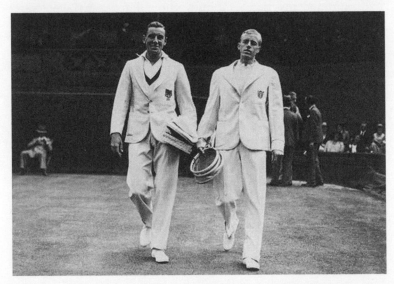

Fred Perry and Sidney Wood at Centre Court at Wimbledon

bet my last marble to beat a guy like Frank, I'd do it. I'd say Borotra couldn't lose to him because Frank was reputed not to have had a backhand and he never passed anybody ever at the net. However, the chemistry of one-on-one matches is something that only those who have been involved in them – and lost at Wimbledon – can ever really comprehend.

The gallery was always normally with Borotra. He was

Wood in action at Wimbledon in 1931

their darling and anything he did, they would rise to laugh with him. But with Frank, he was put down. Not that Frank put him down, but just that Frank's personality was such that it commanded so much of the gallery's interest. Borotra did his routine and changed his beret, which he would do about four or five times a set sometimes. (He had seven berets out there.) He'd change his racquets and rush over and change his beret. This was his game. He'd do it and it would look silly and it would not endear him to the gallery. He felt this, and as a result, he played defensively against Frank. Frank read this too and, for some reason or other, he played sort of disdainfully with Jean. He played shots against him that he wouldn't try to make against me. He'd pass Borotra, who was the greatest volleyer and net-coverer that there ever was in the world. He'd pass Borotra down the line with his screwy violin-bow backhand that he had and, it looked as if he meant it. He passed him consistently.

Leading two-sets-to-one and a service break 4-3 in the fourth set, Frank twisted his knee. It hadn't tightened up on him, so he was still able to serve and win the match. Frank beat Jean 7-5, 3-6, 6-4, 6-4, and we were all set and thrilled to be meeting in the Wimbledon final.

Shields led Borotra two sets to one and serving at 4-3, 40-30 when the infamous injury happened. He slipped on a ball at the net and fell hard to the ground in clear pain, twisting his knee. Borotra ran to the net to help Shields. He held his arm, guided him to the sidelines and brought him water and his coat for comfort. He even began to rub the injured knee of his fallen opponent.

Shields eventually wobbled back to the baseline and attempted to con-

tinue play. So uncertain of the match continuing as Shields limped, the chair umpire needed assurance and asked, "Are you alright, Shields?"

Wrote Ferdinand Kuhn in The New York Times, "The crowd thought it was about to witness a debacle almost at the moment of Shields's victory. Once more, both players left the court, but this time Shields, though still limping, would not hear of a postponement. The Frenchman, still skeptical, ran back to his position, waiting for Shields to finish his service. Shields answer was swift and ruthless when it came."

Shields limped to the line and delivered one mighty unreturnable cannonball serve. Borotra was not able to return the bolt of lightning, and with one swing of the racquet, Shields held serve for a 5-3 lead.

Faced with the prospect of only having to hold serve on his next service game to reach the Wimbledon final, Shields did not put forth any effort as Borotra served the next game, saving his fitness and the risk of further injuring his tender knee. After Borotra held serve easily for 4-5, Shields then served for the final.

Shields fired an ace on his first swing of the racquet. 15-0. Another cannon shot was fired that Borotra got his racquet on, but the Frenchman hit the ball beyond the baseline. 30-0. Shields missed a volley on a sojourn to net on the next point to draw Borotra to 30-15, further confirming that Shields would likely have to win the point outright on the serve if he were to close out the match. After missing a first serve on the next point, Shields was given a gift as Borotra netted the second-serve return, giving Shields double match point at 40-15. All he would need is one more swing of the racquet, blazing another ace past Borotra to close out the dramatic victory.

Wrote Kuhn in The New York Times, "Finally, at match point, a sizzling serve flew past Borotra with the speed of a high velocity shell. The match was over and Shields walked off the court amid one of the greatest and friendliest ovations any American winner has had at Wimbledon."

-David Wood

THE SCENARIO TO US WAS IMPLAUSIBLE. TO BE NOT MUCH over 19 years old, unheedingly optimistic and as unworldly as a hayseed, and along with your doubles partner, roommate and closest chum, at ages 19 and 21, beat Perry and Borotra and gain the 1931 Wimbledon men's singles final. You can imagine our unconfined elation. Here we were, two unheralded near babes in the international tennis woods, who had prevailed, match by match, over the game's towering titans of America, Australia, England and France. To us it was a family victory, for Shields and Wood were as close as Damon and Pythias. For hours after our semifinal victories, we would just stare at each other a minute or two and burst out into cackling, back-thwacking guffaws.

Neither of us took Frank's twisted knee too seriously, even when Sam Hardy, the captain of the U.S. Davis Cup team at the time, told us that Frank should default the final due to his injured knee. Hardy, a very conscientious fella, told us about the cable communication with the peerless powers of the U.S. Lawn Tennis Association (the modern-day U.S. Tennis Association) that had resulted in the decision for Frank to default in order to preserve him for our upcoming Davis Cup match, to be played a fortnight later in Paris.

Frank wanted to play, but maybe there was a little reluctance on both our parts to play also, who knows what it was? We were really too young to stand up for what we thought should be done.

I don't recall our being particularly disturbed, for we had won the title. At that point, flushed with victory and every immature right to believe that this was only the first of many All England Club wins for us, the Wimbledon title was something euphoric for the present, but far more important was the incontrovertible proof that our thousands of hours of practice and our families' sacrifices had earned us a sure toehold on the pinnacle occupied by the Olympians of our cherished sport. Having little awareness of the niceties of Anglo-American relations, it did not then occur to us that our Association's decision was an unthinkable affront to British officialdom, and to fans who had purchased tickets for the final match.

The day after his dramatic semifinal win over Jean Borotra – and two days before the scheduled Wimbledon men's singles final – Frank Shields and my father actually had to play a semifinal doubles match against Henri Cochet and Jacques Brugnon on Centre Court. The Frenchmen

Wood and Shields at Wimbledon, 1931

won the match 6-4, 7-5, 6-2 as Shields struggled with his injured knee.
Wrote The New York Times, *"It was easy to see that Shields was limping
and not able to put up his best game against the Frenchmen, who won
the match."* Lawn Tennis and Badminton *said of the match, "Shields
was handicapped through the injury he sustained to his leg and was slow
about the court. Wood endeavoured to do all the running about but with
one man slow off the mark, their defeat was inevitable."*

On Friday, July 3, the day before the scheduled men's singles final, a
doctor again examined Shields, and U.S. Davis Cup Captain Sam Hardy
told the Wimbledon officials of the default. Late in the afternoon after
the close of play, Allen Gland from the All England Club officially announced the default on behalf of the tournament as Shields' injury "has
not yielded to treatment."

"It's all the luck of the game," said Shields in a statement issued from
the Grosvenor House Hotel. "Of course I am very disappointed, not
only because of the public, but because I might have equaled the record
of (Gerald) Patterson and (Bill) Tilden by winning the championship on
my first attempt. Wood, of course, is even more disappointed than I am,
but with my leg as it is, I wouldn't be able to give him a good game."

Hardy's statement read as follows: "In view of the serious condition
of his leg, Shields will be unable to appear against Wood, and thus de-
faults the match to his fellow country-man."

Play in the Centre Court on the final day of The Championships con-
sisted of the following matches: the women's doubles semifinal match
between Doris Metaxa of France and Josane Sigart of Belgium against
Betty Nuthall and Eileen Whittingstall of Britain, the France-USA men's
doubles final between Cochet-Brugnon vs. Lott-Van Ryn, the women's
doubles final between the British team of Dorothy Shepherd-Barron and
Phyllis Mudford vs. Metaxa and Sigart, the mixed doubles final between
Americans Lott and Anna Harper vs. the British team of Ian Collins-
Joan Ridley followed by the "All England Plate" singles final (the since

discontinued consolation tournament) between Vernon Kirby of South Africa and George Rogers of Ireland.

Sir Francis Gordon Lowe, the former British Davis Cupper, even suggested that Shields should have been defaulted due to a time violation against Borotra. "Personally, as things turned out, it would have been better if Shields had scratched to Borotra when the accident happened," he wrote in The New York Times. *"It was pretty obvious when his knee became stiff that he was going to have difficulty playing the game for at least a week...Technically, as the French captain Pierre Gillou pointed out, Shields ought to have been scratched by the umpire for exceeding the three-minute interval allowed for these stoppages. Otherwise, according to the rules, play must be continued throughout. His scratching has been a great blow to Wimbledon..."*

Ironically, Fred Perry was also forced to unwillingly withdraw from Wimbledon for fear of risking further injury, upon pressure from Britain's Davis Cup captain. Playing in the mixed doubles semifinal on Thursday with Mary Heeley against Lott and Harper, Perry and his partner led 6-1, 4-3 when Perry fell over a linesperson, landing on the concrete that surrounded Court No. 1. He was taken to the locker room for a doctor's observation, where British Davis Cup Captain Herbert Roper-Barrett pulled the plug on him finishing the match, much to his chagrin. Roper Barrett would not have Perry risk further injury that would jeopardize the Davis Cup effort. As American Lawn Tennis *magazine said of Roper-Barrett and Hardy, "Both captains were evidently mindful of the unwritten law that one's duty to one's country comes first."*

The Davis Cup matches in Paris following Wimbledon was the primary reason the U.S. Lawn Tennis Association financed and facilitated the European trip for my father, Shields as well as Lott and John Van Ryn, who paired to beat Cochet and Brugnon to win the Wimbledon doubles title. The team left Wimbledon for Paris on Sunday July 5, providing 12 days of rest and practice on the clay courts at Roland Gar-

ros prior to their Inter-zone Final match against Great Britain, with the winner earning the right to play against the holder France for the Davis Cup title.

Despite my father beating Perry in the Wimbledon semifinals, and Shields' beating Perry's countryman Bunny Austin in the Wimbledon quarterfinals, both British players exacted revenge and swept the final two singles matches of the series to give Britain the 3-2 win. With the United States leading 2-1 on the final day of play, my father lost to Perry 6-3, 8-10, 6-3, 6-3 to square the tie at 2-2, while Shields, after beating Perry on the opening day's singles, lost to Austin 8-6, 6-3, 7-5 in the fifth and decisive match. The U.S. loss meant that for the first time since 1912, the U.S. would field a Davis Cup team that would not compete in the Challenge Round of the competition.

- David Wood

I KNEW THE DAY BEFORE THE SCHEDULED FINAL THAT I WAS the champion. Frank wanted to play, and could have played. But the U.S. Davis Cup committee wouldn't let him.

Can you imagine that happening today, expecting a guy to give up a shot at the Wimbledon title just to be ready for a Davis Cup match? But we were amateurs then, and the USTA had the power of life and death over us. Frank and I thought it was a terrible affront to Wimbledon to leave them without a men's final, but that's the way it was. We felt we were co-champs. Being the Wimbledon champion, it sounds great, but it's a lot of luck. Once you win it once, you think you're going to win it every year because you think it's so easy. It isn't easy at all.

I have no idea what would have happened with me against Frank in the final. It wasn't Frank's fault that he had to default. He didn't really want to default. I know that obviously

I wanted to play, at the same time I figured well, if Frank were to default, I'm the Wimbledon Champion and we'll play it off some other time, which is exactly what we did....

The Wimbledon Renshaw Trophy

• CHAPTER FOUR •

The Private Understanding Playoff

FRANK SHIELDS AND I MADE A PRETTY JUVENILE PACT following Wimbledon in 1931 that whoever won in our next important grass court final should own the priceless Wimbledon Renshaw Trophy that I was awarded by the All England Club for the final-round default of my injured buddy and roommate. It was our "private understanding playoff" to settle the Wimbledon final that was never played.

I asked the stately Maud Barger-Wallach to be custodian of my priceless trophy. As a couple of happily shook up, victorious 19 and 21-year-olds, we assumed that Wimbledon in 1931 would be only the first of numerous big-time finals appearances.

Mrs. Wallach, who was a generation and a half past being the U.S. women's singles champion (she won the title in 1908 at the age of 38!) was the perennial "mascot" of our Davis Cup teams as she'd come over to Europe every year with the U.S. Davis Cup team. She was a great friend of Frank and mine and was sort of the first lady of tennis in Newport, R.I. – a sparkplug really. She would sell off an emerald here and a diamond there to finance some promising youngster's trip to Europe to compete at Paris and Wimbledon. We all loved Mrs. Wallach and she was quite a character. She once conceived the idea of secreting an ice pack beneath her wide-brimmed bonnet that she wore on court to play matches, to remain cool and collected under the mid-summer sun.

So, I gave her the trophy. This was strictly an immature tennis thing, but this is how we did it in those days. I gave her the trophy and it was agreed that she would hold it until Frank and I met in the final of another grass court tournament, someplace, somewhere.

It would be three years before Frank and I gained the final round of the pre-Wimbledon Queens Club tournament in 1934. To top it off, the U.S. Davis Cup Committee designated it as a match to decide which of us would play in the No. 1 position for the United States in the upcoming matches against Australia at the All England Club.

It was the strangest match I had ever played in my life because Frank was a nervous wreck, but I wasn't. I don't know why, but Frank was so tense in this match, and Frank was never a very nervous guy. Apparently this thing meant – not meant more – but it bothered him more. I'm sure Frank felt he shouldn't have defaulted and he probably could have played almost well enough, because the knee was not that bad. It was a risky thing maybe for the possibility of injuring it further, but he felt badly for not playing, for he might have won the tournament. Everybody kind of knew Frank didn't default, he was directed to default, but anyway we didn't look ahead at what was going to show in the record books ten and 20 years from that point. That was the way it was done. At that point, that was a passing thing. We were No. 1 and No. 2 in the world, in the final of Wimbledon, and we'd beaten everybody. I mean, what are you going to say? So, the next year we were no longer No. 1 and No. 2 and we'd both been clobbered a couple of times in the meantime.

So we met in the Queen's Club final and just like that, I jumped to a 5-0, love-40 lead on Frank's serve. I played safely and well. I had a special formula – call it a special way of handling Frank's serve – which was strictly a gamble, but it was the only way to play Frank's serve. If you didn't gamble, he aced you many, many times.

Incidentally, as an aside, in one summer of tennis, it was the summer after the Wimbledon default in 1931, Frank won some crazy thing like five Eastern grass court tournaments, and Allison Danzig of *The New York Times* kept a record of Frank's aces in every match, I think from the quarterfinals on, and Frank averaged something like 2.38 clean aces per game. I don't mean on errors, clean aces that were not touched on his first serve in all those matches. Now, this is quite a feat – 2.38 aces per every service game. Anyway, Frank didn't average this against me because I would go to the side that I'd expect him to serve – well, hoped that he would serve to – and his serve came so hard that if you were there and your reflexes were good, you could make a better return than you normally would on people. If you were wrong, he's going to serve the ace anyway, so it makes no difference if you were there on one side or the other, or the middle of the court. The ace would be an ace. He hit the chalk more than anybody in the world.

So Frank was serving at love-40 and, all up at once, his nervousness disappeared. There wasn't anything to lose at that point and he served five clean aces. Four of these were on first serves and one was on a second serve. He hit the chalk on five straight points.

Frank's crunchers were certifiably the most consistently accurate of all first serves. He wasted no time with preliminaries or flourishes in his swing. He would simply ease the racquet to a cocked position, like a pitcher with a runner on base, and blow in his strikes with effortless precision.

Don Budge could also tell you something about Frank's delivery. He played Frank only once, which was in Frank's over-the-hill, last competitive year, and when Don walked into the Newport locker room after prevailing in a 6-4 fifth set match, I asked him how come he looked so bushed. He said, "I spent three-and-a-half hours out there with my knees bent so I could move either way to block Frank's bullets and it's the first time in my life my legs ever ached."

After Frank's ace-laden escape to avoid losing the first set 6-0, I then dropped my serve, got the elbow, and bang-bang, and suddenly it was 5-5. I ultimately squeezed out the win 11-9, 6-0. Jack Crawford, the great Australian player, later informed me that I had been clean-aced 11 times in Frank's three service games from 0-5.

I lucked out in what you can believe was a pretty tense match. It took Mrs. Wallach a month to withdraw my trophy from her safe deposit box. She was fond of me, but she adored Frank!

Frank died in 1975, and though it was something I had been prepared for, it affected me terribly. After the funeral in Southampton, I went home, had two Bloody Marys and decided to write an obituary for my lifetime buddy. Here is the way Frank would have liked it to have said:

"The flag at the Meadow Club of Southampton hung at half mast on the day that Francis Xavier Shields was being buried. Frank's heart, as warm and stubborn as any that ever beat, after several near-misses, finally gave out on Tuesday night, August 19, 1975.

Frank's exploits in international tennis assured him a place as one of the titans of his era, indeed of all time. Ranked No. 1 in the United States in 1933, he was ranked in the first five in the U.S. rankings six times and in the top ten in the U.S. eight times. He also ranked among the world's top ten five times. He played on four of our Davis Cup teams and served as the U.S. Davis Cup captain in 1951. He was enshrined in the International Tennis Hall Of Fame in 1964. His abilities exceeded his exploits, however notable, but Frank's training habits, which only his extraordinary constitution could survive, were obstacles to even more stellar accomplishments.

The record is there for all to read. What's missing are the events which made Frank a never-to-be-forgotten legend in his time. Only a well remembered few are recounted here. Frank,

Wood and Shields off the tennis court

a 6'4" all-sports gifted athlete, could palm a basketball in either hand and shoot with the best. Name the sport and he did it effortlessly and professionally. In the view of everyone who has ever faced Frank's first serve – it was the greatest ever hit. In one Ripley-like demonstration in France for a $100 prize for the most hits out of a hundred on a 24" square target placed in an optional service box corner, Frank hit an incredible 56 consecutive serves on the plate – and 67 overall. His Davis Cup teammates, George Lott, Johnny Van Ryn and myself among them, amassed just 39 out of our combined 300 tries.

With his Gary Cooper looks and unconsciously irresistible charm, Frank was the gallery favorite. Sam Goldwyn put him under contract, but Frank was too much Frank to become an actor. Instead, he talked Goldwyn and Harry Cohn of Columbia Pictures into test-screening Errol Flynn, but with no success. He then convinced Jack Warner that he'd better look over Errol pretty fast because Goldwyn and Cohn were hot after him. Next scene, eight weeks later, Errol lands the lead in *Captain Blood* and he's on his way.

No athlete has evoked more admiration, adulation and sheer disbelief on and off the court than Frank Shields. Surely he is the only man, before or since, who would cross the ocean to Paris for the French Championship and, following an over-extended celebration, find himself aboard the *SS Paris* en route home with only a dinner jacket for luggage.

The overworked word, "charisma," came much later than my unforgettable, beloved friend 'Shultzie.' But if ever a term was formed to fit a man, that man was Frank Shields."

CHAPTER FIVE

From Wimbledon To Wall Street

THE YEAR WAS 1931. THE STOCK MARKET WAS AT ITS nadir, and a 1/8 uptick on a stock was far more important than the services of a newly-crowned Wimbledon champion. Each day, I would rattle into Manhattan from St. James (Long Island) in an old tin Lizzie Ford to seek my fortune, more accurately, in hopes of contributing something to my family's depression-dwindled income.

After weeks of getting no further than the waiting rooms of numerous brokerage houses, it became increasingly clear that firing, not hiring, was the prevailing way of life on Wall Street. Among the macabre jokes going the rounds was that firms were installing diving boards on their windowsills.

Then one day when I called home, there was a message from an older Memphis friend, Brigadier General A.K. Tigrett. The message said that he was in town and would like me to have dinner with him and stay over at the Vanderbilt Hotel (the tennis people's digs at the time). A.K. was the President of the Southern Tennis Association, as well as the Cottonseed Oil Company of Memphis.

A.K. noticed that I was not my normally ebullient self, and when I told him of my job-hunt frustrations, he immediately said not to worry and that he'd fix me up the next day! So in the company of two of A.K.'s young Ziegfeld Follies charmers, we went out to dine and dance.

The next morning, ring around the collar and all, A.K. took me downtown to meet Dick Hoyt of Hayden Stone, then a major brokerage firm. I was immediately put to work as a runner at the going rate of $8 per week (about $250 in today's money). Only those who were around back then could appreciate what it meant for me to bring home my first-ever paycheck. I can truthfully say that it was more rewarding than being presented with Wimbledon's treasured Renshaw winner's trophy.

The next summer, the USLTA somehow managed to provide enough expense funds for my Wimbledon defense junket to cover what I'd be missing from working at Hayden Stone.

Come the following September when, after a tough loss in the semifinals of Forest Hills, I headed for Long Island and the house of George F. Baker, whose daughter, Titi, had indicated I'd be welcome. Tommy Suffern Tailer, a friend and top golfer (known to intimates as T. Suffering Cats), was married to Titi's sister Flo. He understood how hard the afternoon's loss had hit me, and made sure that I was provided a few extra quaffs to assuage my loss.

The next morning with throbbing head, I boarded Mr. Baker's commuter cruiser for the trip to New York. Mr. Baker headed National City Bank, and my fellow passengers were a half dozen other high-level tycoons. When a huge tureen of scrambled eggs and bacon appeared, I paled, excused myself and managed to survive the voyage.

When we arrived at "my" 25 Broad Street office, who should pull up but Charles Hayden, head of the firm. Mr. Baker introduced us, and in the elevator, when Mr. Hayden asked, "What floor?" and I replied, "Nine," he exclaimed, "That's one of mine!" Not more than ten minutes later, I was told to report to the tenth floor where to my astonishment, a desk awaited me with a note that I was now a "Customer's Man" at the then un-heard of munificence of $25 per day! My job seeking sequence sure added credence to the "It's not what but who you know" adage. (Charles Hayden was also the power behind the Waldorf Astoria funding that got it built.)

About a year later, yet another A.K. favor: He called to tell me that the Gulf Mobile and Ohio Railroad, headed by his brother, I.B., would be paying a whopping $18 in accumulat-ed dividends, on its $50 par value convertible preferred. The stock hadn't yet moved and I loaded family and everyone up to the hilt at its 38 to 40 sub-par price. Only a couple of weeks later, the entire $18 back interest was paid and the ex-divi-dend price jumped up to near its $50 par value. The combined back interest and ten or so point stock appreciation netted us close to a 100 percent profit. There was then no Securities & Exchange Commission, and no perception that insider tips weren't entirely kosher. So, double bless you, A.K.

René Lacoste

CHAPTER SIX

My Favorite Match

THE CHOICE OF MY FAVORITE MATCH IS DIFFICULT. MY thoughts wander back across 22 years of international competition (I first played on the Centre Court at Wimbledon against world champion René Lacoste when I was only 15) and memory lights on at least a dozen matches that I'd never want to forget. Quite naturally, most of these were skirmishes in which I was the victor. But the match that towers above all others in my mind is one that I lost.

In 1932, the International Club sent me to Paris for the French Championships. The seeding was to bring me against Lacoste in the semifinals. René, after two years of ill health and retirement, had entered this tournament as his initial "comeback" effort with the hope of eventually regaining his world championship. I was the Wimbledon champion of the year before. When Lacoste ground down his first four opponents in 12 sets with a total loss of only four games against such resolute competitors as Spain's Enrique Maier, among others, I began remembering the fear of his invincibility which I had had since the age of 15. It's no wonder I was half petrified for a whole week at our approaching meeting in the semis. Furthermore, I was not a master of playing on the French red clay. In fact, I barely staggered through my bracket with full-limit matches against less worthy opposition.

For those who never had a chance to see Lacoste play tennis, let me say that his was a classically perfect game. Imagine a player who never came to the net beating Borotra in his prime on fast wood boards 6-4, 6-0, 6-4 in one of our National Indoor finals. Though René was the steadiest player I've ever seen or heard of, his accuracy and deception gave him a devastating attack as well.

When our match began, I started right after him, taking the net on good length and volleying sharply. At the end of 20 minutes, the score was 6-0, 6-1, 4-0—but not in my favor. At this moment, all I could think of was what the headlines would look like in America the next morning. In those better-promoted days, tennis did make the headlines!

I remember at 0-4 turning my back on René for a full minute while I swore to my immortal soul that I'd stay in the back-court and "outfloat" him and win just one more game— or it would be my last match!

Then it began. The "first" game took probably ten minutes. I won it, stayed with the same formula and won another. An hour later, still unbelieving, the set was mine, 9-7. Another hour, another 10,000 balls crossing the net, and I was even with him, winning the fourth set 8-6!

The fifth set went along like a six-day bike race with hardly more than a point separating us at any time. Finally (like people who are seasick and no longer care if they die—so long as it's soon) we no longer cared who won, both of us simply hoping to be on our feet at the end. It came, mercifully, with René winning the last point and the set at 8-6. For an hour afterwards we lay on adjoining rubbing tables, each with cramps and contortions of every known muscle.

Why is this my favorite match? Because it taught me a lesson I've never forgotten. I'm proud to pass this on here. I set my mind on winning a game, and almost came out with the match. No matter how faulty your purpose may be, if you do have that purpose and hold to it tenaciously, things must swing your way.

CHAPTER SEVEN

Doing Laundry With Don Budge and Arnold Palmer

IN 1939, I THOUGHT I'D LIKE TO TRY SOMETHING WHERE the value of a name in sport could be exploited in a competitive business, where the name would have a greater value than "Mr. Smith." I looked into different businesses that were essential to people's lives and I picked the laundry business.

I started it with Frank Shields because I thought it would be nothing but a laughingstock, so I said, "Frank, let's get laughed at together," and it was an instant success. Frank was otherwise involved in the insurance business and was asked by his bosses to drop the laundry pursuits, so he dropped out and Don Budge came in. Don was a great friend of mine and somewhat a protegé in a sense. I believe Don would have confirmed that it was I who got him to change from a Western forehand to an Eastern forehand. I was the one who actually initiated with the U.S. Lawn Tennis Association that Don should travel with the U.S. Davis Cup team that first year when they weren't going to take him. Don actually replaced me on the team, so maybe I shouldn't have been so generous!

Anyway, we went into business with the idea that Don would open us in California, but Don got much more involved in professional tennis after winning the Grand Slam in 1938 and really didn't have an opportunity to do this. However, it turned into a terrific success (one of our slogans was "Rub-a-dub-dub, Budge-Wood have a tub") and subsequently I introduced the idea to golfing legend Arnold Palmer and his camp.

The first time I met up with Arnie was in the bar of a Philadelphia Marriot Inn near the Whitemarch Club where he was playing in a tournament. It was essentially a business meeting, but undoubtedly there would be sporting overtones. My wife Pat was there, as was Arnie's Winnie and his chum, super-agent head of International Management Group, Mark McCormack.

When I dreamed up the idea of setting up a marquee name, national franchise laundry and dry cleaning chain, there was no question that Arnie's name was far and away the one that would sell the best. So I called Mark, who was interested and asked me to meet with him. A couple of days later when I

Sidney Wood with Arnold Palmer

knocked on the hotel door, it flung open and this guy points his finger at me and hollers, "I saw you beat Frankie Parker in Chicago!" That was my introduction to Mark McCormack, and you can say I liked his style!

I asked Arnie if he ever hoisted one during a tournament, and he said, "One after a good round; and two if it was a lousy day." That afternoon it was just the pro-am, and Arnie, a Pennsylvanian to the core, asked for a boilermaker and looked at me. I nodded, and after another round there was little talk of business and much comparing of golf and tennis play and players. We ended up founding the Arnold Palmer Cleaning Centers, which was an immediate success and was subsequently sold out among some of Arnold's other enterprises.

Wrote McCormack in *Sports Illustrated* in 1967, "What Sidney Wood knew, and we all learned, was that if two dry cleaning shops are going to open in the same block and one is called Arnold Palmer and the other is Jack Smith's, it is the Palmer shop that a new customer is more likely to try."

CHAPTER EIGHT

Dave Selznick

DAVE SELZNICK, THE RENOWNED HOLLYWOOD PRODUCER, and his terrific wife Irene, daughter of Hollywood's all-powerful Louis B. Mayer of Metro Goldwyn Mayer (MGM), were regulars at Charlie Chaplin's bi-weekly Sunday breakfasts, invariably followed by a stint on the court with some strange matchups. At one such set-to, an errant shot of Charlie's shattered Dave's glasses with quite a bit of bloodshed and some shards that seemed to be in a pupil. Charlie was jumping around like a decapitated chicken, but Dave was reassuring everyone and laughing at his slow reflexes. Fred Perry and I drove him to the hospital where he spent the night and was fine.

Dave would throw himself birthday parties, most often at New York's El Morocco, with about a dozen friends, and it was one invite I'd never pass up. When his big winner, *Gone with the Wind*, opened, guess who was front and center?

Sidney Wood with Gary Cooper

CHAPTER NINE

Shooting it up with Gary Cooper

APART FROM BEING AN INVETERATE TENNIS DEVOTEE, Gary Cooper, the Academy-award winning tough-guy actor, was an enthusiastic gunslinger. His ravishing wife Rocky wasn't bad either, having been numero uno in California skeet shooting for five straight years. So it was no surprise, visiting them in Tucson, to have Gary march out a brand new pair of pearl-handled pistols and head for an orange grove to try them out.

A Coke bottle was set up on a branch, and Gary and Rocky fired away without success. I was never better than a poorish pistoleer so when Gary handed over one of the guns, I didn't bother to take aim and fired away from the hip. My first shot blasted the bottle to smithereens. Gary and Rocky were agape, but I just blew into the muzzle and handed the gun back to Gary and was smart enough to refuse all demands to repeat my Calamity Jane performance.

The trip wasn't a total success because I was less lucky in purchasing a pair of hard-starched Levis to go bareback riding, the only way I'd done it in my earlier Arizona home-steading days. But that was ten years before, and I ate dinner standing up.

In those days (late 1930s and early 1940s), Hollywood was

a relatively small community where everyone in the film industry and its fringes knew one another on a nickname basis. My mining offices were on Sunset Boulevard, just where the then existing Beverly Hills bridle path began, and since my street level co-tenant was Jack Morgan's much-in-vogue Cock 'n Bull restaurant, I had quite few visitors around lunch hour.

One day, Gary came by and wished he hadn't. Our office staff was about to have a coffee-break softball game on a neighboring lot and Gary came along. He was handed the bat and proceeded to hit a slow grounder toward first base. When the first baseman (our bookkeeper), whose name I mercifully omit, saw the God-like Cooper descending on him, he completely blew his cool and hurled the ball at Gary, blasting him right between the eyes. Gary went down like a felled oak, and we thought for a moment that it was bad news. Thankfully, he wasn't seriously hurt, but I doubt if either our demoralized accountant or Coop had any inclination to play baseball for a spell.

When Gary later starred as Lou Gehring in *Pride of the Yankees*, I asked him if he were ever haunted by his earlier beaning. He just gave me one of those quirk-mouth Cooper looks.

When my first wife Edith and I would pick up Gary and Rocky (a girlhood schoolmate of Edith's) to go out for dinner and dancing, the ladies would repair to the boudoir to prink up; and Gary, who was no boozer but appreciated male conviviality, would pour us a healthy belt of scotch and say, "Here's to sin." This was unfailingly the same Gary you see on film and always game to try anything that looked like fun.

One time, when a couple of our new, brightly emblazoned Budge-Wood Service trucks (yes, that was my Sidney Wood,

Don Budge Laundry, etc. enterprise) were delivered to our Manhattan plant, Gary happened to be visiting me. I said, "Let's go," so the boys loaded up one of the trucks and Gary and I took off, with Gary making front door deliveries to some incredulous clients.

CHAPTER TEN

The Other Errol

IT WOULDN'T BE EASY FOR THOSE WHO HAVE BEEN exposed to the later years' sad portrait of the hopelessly dissolute Errol Flynn to believe that when he arrived in Hollywood, he was well read, well bred, socially desirable, and a witty and considerate companion. Apart from Olympic swimmer Johnny Weissmuller, he was also the movie colony's only first-rate athlete.

I first ran across the swashbuckling actor at the L.A. Tennis Club, where Errol would appear with bowler hat, bumbershoot and a black cocker spaniel on a leash. He could not then afford to be a member, but would come around partly because he loved tennis, but mostly in hopes of running into a director or producer (in which the club abounded) who might give him some "extra" work as a valet, butler or anything that would earn him a day's wages. There were more than a few nights when Frank Shields (then under contract to Sam Goldwyn) or I would take Errol home to dinner just so he wouldn't go hungry.

During the several years that we saw a lot of each other, there was not the slightest hint that alcohol, and later drugs, would eventually be his undoing. Of all the male stars of that era, more adulation was heaped on Errol than any other, including Robert Taylor, Tyrone Power and Clark Gable. If only his good looks and personality were matched by the ability to occasionally say "No!"

When my business took me from New York to California, which then had been practically a "milk run" for me, I most often stayed with the famed Canadian actor Walter Pidgeon, and, however surprisingly, the first night in town would be a strictly stag get-together dinner with Errol at Dave Chasen's, The Brown Derby, Cock 'n Bull or Romanoff's. Despite ear-whispered invitations from passing ladies, Errol didn't succumb. I don't know when he began to lose the battle of self-indulgence, because shortly after we teamed up for a U.S. Championship qualifying doubles tournament in Santa Barbara (that was in 1940, just before World War II shut down my "war non-essential" mining operations.) I closed

Errol Flynn

our Beverly Hills office and moved east.

At Santa Barbara, Errol and I were accompanied by his wife, the French beauty Lili Damita, to whom Frank Shields had introduced Errol. For the record, Flynn and yours truly knocked off some pretty high-level teams to reach the final and actually qualify for the U.S. Nationals, the modern-day US Open. Errol played amazingly well under fire. Thinking back, his was an extraordinary performance for one whose experience was limited to club practice play. We never thought seriously about going to Boston for the Nationals, but wouldn't it have been great if we had?

Errol and Lili argued a bit; that is, Lili argued and Errol stayed silent as long as he could. On this trip, she finally got to him – via Robert Donat – taunting Errol that he couldn't do as much with a whole script as Donat could do with one eyebrow. This was in our joint Santa Barbara sitting room, and I decamped as Errol was about to gag Lili with a pair of just-pulled-off wet tennis socks.

Back in New York, Errol and I got together whenever he came east until he started to go to seed. The next time I saw him was after no contact for at least a decade, during which Errol had gone to Cuba and met and supported Castro and his revolution. My fourth wife Pat and I were being shown to our table at Manhattan's El Morocco and Errol was moving up the aisle in our direction. I said carefully, "Hello, Errol, this is Pat." Errol kissed her hand, clapped me jovially on the shoulder and said something like "Hello buddy" without a flicker of recognition. Though prepared to see a forlorn facsimile of my one-time pal, this pathetically witless wreck of a man gave me a rotten night.

CHAPTER ELEVEN

Scarecrow Server

IN WHAT SEEMS TO BE A NATURAL FORM OF GREETING to tennis players from bartenders, maitre d's, orchestra leaders and certain friends, I was often saluted with a forehand or backhand swipe, but none as energetically as by the *Wizard of Oz*'s Ray Bolger. When the ever-ebullient man best known as the scarecrow would spy me, he would leap to his feet and swing madly at an imaginary lob, picking up a soupspoon or other utensil for his racquet. He may not have had the greatest overhead in the world, but he would certainly guarantee you a well-announced entrance at "21" or El Morocco.

Ray and I agreed that our dolichocephalic visages were similarly handsome, and one night at the old Stork Club, when a photographer took aim at my maiden fair seated at a banquette, Ray slid in next to her and said to the cameraman, "Guess which one's the tennis player." With his fabulous footwork and some serious practice with his soupspoon, who knows!

CHAPTER TWELVE

Near Immortality at Grauman's Chinese Theatre

TOURNAMENT TENNIS COMPETITORS ARE NO STRANGERS to the roller coaster rise and fall of fortune, from the high excitement of victory to the near-inconsolable depths of defeat. But an experience that crossed my path at age 17 was a useful early lesson in just how rapidly a burgeoning pouter pigeon ego can suffer overnight deflation. It occurred, of all places, at Grauman's Chinese Theatre in Hollywood, where practically all the big movie "first nights" were then staged.

At the grand opening of the world's very first talkie-musical *Broadway Melody* starring Joan Crawford and Eddie Cantor, I had the excruciating honor of serving as squire to the show's featured starlet, Miss Anita Page, whose dazzling blonde beauty graced the covers of myriad movie magazines. Anita was also 17 and a real live Wampus Baby Star (Hollywood's then equivalent of a junior Davis Cup squadder).

Looking back at what seems like another age, I remember the blinding Klieg lights, hordes of screaming idolaters and everyone darting around like so many hummingbirds among a surfeit of nectared flowers. Alighting from our MGM limousine, with the unattainable queen of my dreams at my side, I was intoxicatingly out of touch with reality. Anita, who must have been rehearsed for this amazing plunge into hysteria, would not let us be severed, as cameras flashed and microphones were stacked before her.

As we slowly advanced up the canopied entrance walk, Anita, swain on arm, was ushered across the theatre's plaza to the roped off, hallowed sanctum where footprints of the heroes and heroines of the silver screen were cast in concrete cemented relief. A tuxedoed gentleman helped Anita off with a shoe and stocking, but, sweetly thoughtful girl that she was, she insisted that my foot too be encased side by side with her own dainty imprint for all posterity. The movie was interrupted from time to time by waves of applause, as the performers first appeared on screen, and I was aglow with a vicarious thrill as Anita's resounding ovation enveloped us.

The next morning's papers were devoured for pictures, but they had cropped off all but your unfamous hero's elbow. Never mind. Fairly early, I summoned my cohort of tennis pals to foregather at Grauman's to view friend Sidney's claim to enduring fame. What a shocker! Overnight, a heartless mason, perhaps anticipating Hollywood's future real estate escalation, had troweled over my immortal sole, leaving Anita's delicate alfresco arch without its protector. Why, oh why, couldn't they have waited just one more day?

Some years later, Anita who had retired from pictures to marry a Navy Captain and become a San Diego housewife, read in the local sports page that I was playing in the Pacific Southwest tournament in Los Angeles, and she drove up to say hello and watch some tennis. Because I seated the coruscant Anita in a front row box, few of the stadium spectators' eyes were focused on the match in progress.

CHAPTER THIRTEEN

Charlie Chaplin in Wonderland

IT IS RARE THAT ONE IS PRIVILEGED TO WITNESS MANI-
fest genius at work. In the late 1930s, when my wife Edith and
I spent the winters in Beverly Hills, a form of charades known
as "The Game" was in vogue for many months at dinner parties, which were frequent in those less-fragmented movie loca-
tion days. The guests would invariably repair to choose up
sides for this pursuit, and with the writing, directing and acting talent that was always present, the subjects chosen and the
performances rendered were anything but run-of-the-mill.

One night at our house, a particular act mesmerized the entire room. Charlie Chaplin came to dinner with his wife Paulette Goddard and wanted to play "The Game" for the first
time. As captain of the opposing team, I presented him with,
of all things, Carroll's "impossible" to act out, "Twas brillig
and the slithy toves did gyre and gimble in the wabe."

Charlie gave his *Alice in Wonderland* slip a brief glance and
disdaining the usual preliminary 'category' signals, proceeded
to somehow create an image that led his team to guess the Jab-
berwocky phrase in seconds. It was a form of unpremeditated
art that defies description, and mystified me for years.

Although Charlie never really had any close men chums, we
became friendly and when he said he would much like to see

an operating gold mine, we went on a three-day jaunt to the Mother Lode region. The first occasion I'd had to observe the public's impression of Charlie as a huge celebrity was when we stopped in Mojave, Calif., (population of about 200 in the day), and before we finished breakfast, there must have been 210 people inside and outside shaking his hand and gawking. In Beverly Hills, Edith and I would have fortnightly breakfast

Charlie Chaplin

for about 30 people at Charlie's, and that sure kept you in the swim in Hollywood.

On the funny side, one day I rang the Chaplin doorbell and Charlie opened the door. I said, "Charlie, I always wanted to ask you where you got that wonderful three-story pipe organ in the foyer." Charlie said, "Aimée gave that to me" (That would be Aimée Semple McPherson, the evangelist who was every bit as famous then as Billy Graham is today—and who had been an inamorata of Charlie's). However, Paulette then appeared and said, "Don't believe a word of it, he bought it at auction."

A couple of years later, I'd flown out to play in the Pacific Southwest tournament in L.A. and asked Paulette if she would like to take me to the tennis in her open-roof Rolls Royce so I could earn some points being seen in her company (also, not everybody had a Rolls in those times!). When we got to the L.A. Tennis Club, I drove around the block several times to make sure everybody got a good look.

When Charlie invited me to the opening of his *Monsieur Verdoux* in New York, I accepted with some reservation because Charlie was not all that funny off-screen, and I was afraid I'd be sitting near him and not be able to laugh enough. After the first three minutes, I was holding my stomach for cramps—he was so damn funny.

I'd have given my soul if I could ever get ahold of a two or three minute short that Charlie filmed with Frank Shields and me. Charlie kept coming out to us on the court with four racquets under his arm as if to join the play and we kept shoving him away. When all's said and done, it's pretty darn nice to have spent quite a few hours in the company of the world's forever great, revered entertainer.

• CHAPTER FOURTEEN •

Replay with Fay Wray

I ONCE RAN ACROSS KING KONG'S MAIN GIRLFRIEND FAY Wray leaving the General Motors Building in New York City, radiant in an ankle length sable. I grabbed her arm and we waltzed across to The Plaza for a cup of tea, babbling away about happy Hollywood memories. Fay said, "When I'm in New York I look at the Empire State Building as though it belongs to me or is it vice-versa?"

In her autobiography *On the Other Hand* she discusses not only her role as the heroine in Merian Cooper's classic production of *King Kong*, but also tells the tale of the pingpong party she hosted at which I beat her using a bedroom slipper for a paddle!

Fay Wray

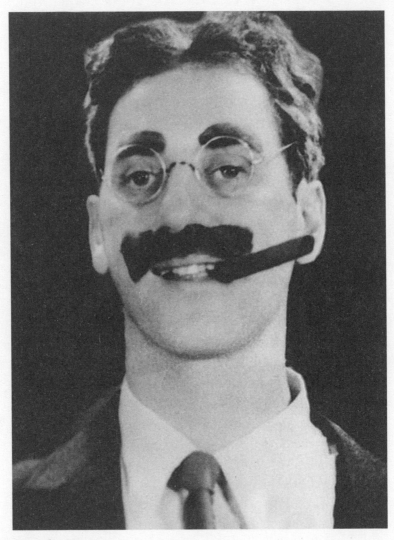

Groucho Marx

CHAPTER FIFTEEN

Groucho Gets Bagged

IN THIS CASE, GROUCHO MARX, THE WORLD'S GREATEST dish-it-outer, showed he could take it. I had arrived at Fred Perry's and Ellsworth Vines' newly acquired Beverly Hills Tennis Club from my Inyo County sulphur property to play an exhibition, along with Frank Shields, to open the club, which Fred was to head up. Groucho and Charlie Chaplin, two tennis dedicatees, were also going to put on a show of doubles with us (those days it was all for fun and friendship.)

I thought it would make an interesting entrance to bring Groucho onto the court in my sleeping bag which I kept in my gear for mining trips. So we put him in the bag, closed the zipper, and Frank slung him over his shoulder and carried him out. I had neglected to tell Groucho that the bag was laden with our refinery's sulphur dust which, while not harmful, would cause me to gush a tear or two before going to sleep.

While the umpire was making the announcement, there were stirrings and muffled sounds emanating from the bag, but I motioned to Frank to ignore them until the umpire was finished. When Groucho was finally released, tears were streaming down his cheeks, and he thought I had gassed him for life. He grabbed a racquet and chased me around the court as the crowd howled in laughter.

CHAPTER SIXTEEN

J. Donald Budge

THIS CRAMOISIE-CROPPED GRAND SLAMMER MADE HIS contemporaries feel like welterweights going against a heavyweight.

Don's trenchant serve was a major weapon, but probably the single most ravaging stroke the game had seen was his prodigious backhand. Clubbed with a 16-1/2 ounce, Paul Bunyan bat (just try wielding one sometime), the basically flat-hit shot would sear the turf and devastate defenses.

You had to overplay a lot of returns to stay with the great Budge. When Don was serving, whether he came up or stayed way back, most of us felt we had to go for broke on most returns or be buried by the weight of his next hit. This meant taking just too many chances, and though you can get lucky for an occasional service break, the percentages always caught up.

Except for a very few exceptional second-servers of the era such as Ellsworth Vines, Gottfried von Cramm, Jack Kramer and Pancho Gonzales, serve and volley tactics against Budge were strictly Russian roulette. You would hear even Jack Kramer, the original serve-volley master, say that while Budge, fellow American Frank Kovacs and Australian John Bromwich were three guys he wouldn't go in against consistently, Don was by far the roughest of the three. Against almost anyone, the serve-volley player, which most of us were in my generation, figures to have an 80 percent chance of holding service, particularly on grass. Even from love-40, you would expect to win a good percentage of service games.

But against Don, it was another ballgame. If you didn't get your first one in, it left you two evil choices: go in and pray you wouldn't get stripped, or stay back and prepare to scramble. From most receivers, you can force a chipped or high backhand, and a reasonably deep first volley lets you close in or force a juicy lob. With Budge, you had to almost always go for the low odds, an extra hard punch or be blunderbussed by his return.

I played every big player around for almost a quarter of a century, from the time I was fifteen, and even long past my serious tennis days, and I have felt reasonably in control of things when I served, and well in the match when receiving. But on my best days, Don - and only Don - could make me, and all but one or two others, feel he was a clear rung above us on the ladder.

There was a side to Budge other than that seen by spectators when he was in all his majesty. Don was someone who'd rather relax than work, but was always ready to work at fun and games. He was witty, entertaining and, on occasions, downright playful. All in all, a nicer fellow to have around than play against.

To go back a way, I first noticed Don at the Berkeley Tennis Club, where he was trailing after his big brother Lloyd like a Rhode Island Red baby chick, carrying a racquet that looked huge because he was so tiny. Both were red-thatched, and Lloyd, at 17, could have put his carbon copy brother of 11 in his pocket.

The next time I saw this baby chick he was all rooster. It was at New Jersey's Orange Lawn Tennis Club where I had reluctantly agreed to give up a weekend to play the annual East-West matches. I was always pretty nice to the newcomers and particularly when they were from my early days' club, as Don quite shyly reminded me that he was. I started off gently with him – too gently. Before I could realize that this crazy looking, skinny kid was actually a backhand disguised as a man, it was too late to recover and he took me.

On Don's first trip east from his Oakland home, he was 18 and his game showed the potential it was later to realize. In that year's U.S. Nationals, he looked like such a sure comer that I went right to the USA's Davis Cup Committee and told them they couldn't leave him off the next year's squad. I told them that with another year of seasoning, beginning with Wimbledon in June, he would be a shoo-in for one of the singles berths the following year. Had I only known how fast Don was to mature, I might not have been so insistent – for Don took my place as one of the two singles players that same first season. Of course, Don went on to achieve many glories on the tennis court, becoming the first player to win the Grand Slam in 1938, sweeping all four major singles titles.

CHAPTER SEVENTEEN

Roof Top Tennis In Manhattan–The Founding of Town Tennis Club

IN 1952, WITH THE INCREASE IN BUILDING IN NEW YORK City fast decimating its numerous empty-lot tennis courts, I got the urge to look into the possibility of utilizing open rooftop areas to save Manhattan's tennis mavens from settling for racquetball. I knew of no previous exploration of this concept and concentrated my survey on primarily lower buildings.

I could go on ad nauseam, but the final result was the fortuitous discovery of the one time, two-story Doelger Brewery in the upscale Sutton Place area of Manhattan. The street-level space owned by Bill Doelger was occupied by the FBI for a garage on 56th Street. An even luckier find was that the three hi-rise apartment houses that bordered the site to the north and east could not be built on.

Bill immediately saw that a four-court, live action tennis landscape, center-pieced by a remodeled, glass-encased second floor of the brewery as a clubhouse and outer terrace, would be a unique, scenic enhancement for his present and projected buildings. My layout design for a not-for-profit club went straight to his architects, who advised that among the multiple code violations that the project would face, the Doelger's East 56th Street apartment entrance – the only feasible entry we could have for the club – was a no-chance approval item. It looked like curtains for us.

But having recruited New York's Mayor, my friend Bob Wagner, as one of our club's governors, I asked him if there was any kind of hardship plea worth pursuing. Bob guffawed and said, "Sid, the city needs tennis courts." I immediately phoned Bill Doelger who said he wanted to kiss me.

So this and multiple other ensuing code violations were summarily quashed and after phoning the Mayor's secretary, Mary, a few times for his signature in response to the NYC Building Department code violations, she suggested that I simply initial his name!

I'm reasonably certain that ours was the first-ever rooftop tennis installation, and at present day is still in business. Some of my purist tennis pals may look upon me as a rules and regulation "Benedict Arnold" for the liberties I took to squeeze four courts into an area that was never intended to accommodate them. With 100 feet of width (half a block) to fit pairs of side-by-side, playable doubles courts and leave enough room for the fencing and for the fat lady to pass between the net posts, called for a bit of nimble doings. It came down to cutting nine inches off each outside alley line, (from 4 ft. 6 in. to 3 ft. 9 in). It's hard to believe, but year after year nobody, including a succession of top-level players on the Church Cup team, the senior version of the Davis Cup, ever had a clue. Sorry about that, fellows!

With the club humming, my wife Pat suggested that we add a 40 by 80 foot ice rink atop our sitting room, aeons before the Donald Trump-built Central Park skating area came into existence. Even Olympic gold medal winner Dick Button would occasionally drop by for a sunny day spin.

CHAPTER EIGHTEEN

The Full Count

AT A PRECOCIOUS BUT DIMINUTIVE 15, I WAS SHIPPED all the way from Arizona to France, in those prehistoric days a two-week junket by train followed by a slow boat, to begin my conquest of the continent's tennis arenas, commencing with the French Championships in Paris. I was billeted in Auteuil with my wonderful aunt Pauline Washburn, whose four children were beginning to talk French like born Bretons. This was my first exposure to the European tennis scene and its habitués, and it was something to remember.

At that time, there were perhaps 30 first-rate players in the French Championships field of 128. At Wimbledon, the number would rise to perhaps 40 (by comparison, the modern 128-man draw has practically no pushovers.) The added starters of those days included a number of truly colorful characters who were competent, often troublesome opponents on the slow European red clay but who had no illusions about their prospects of attaining immortality. Many had independent means, however slender, and the relatively brief season was, to them, a convivial sporting occasion during which they could reunite with their tennis colleagues and visit other friends at the various tournament stops.

One tall, dark and inseparable pair was Nicolai Mishu, ambassador-at-large from Romania, who often on an afternoon appeared in swallow-tailed embassy regalia replete with red ribbon angled across his chest, and his doubles partner and pal, Count Ludwig Salm Von Hoogsträten, who had become enamored of an American girl, Millicent Rogers, who was finishing school in Paris, and had married her there. Her father had considerable interests in oil (Standard Oil) but as we later relate, somewhat less in foreign sons-in-law.

Ludwig, or "Luddy" as he instructed me to call him, appointed himself my sponsor, which included introducing me to the most expensive eating establishments of Paris, of course as his guest, where I would marvel at the surrounding elegances. Always there would be two breathtakingly glamorous ladies, one for Luddy, one for Nicolai, and while their conversation was often a melange of strange foreign tongues, I reveled in every word. My champagne goblet was kept at brim with sparkling ginger ale, and the cigars, though regretted, were always proffered. In short, Luddy, Mishu and their ladies unfailingly treated me as a mature cosmopolite, and I loved them for it.

The night following my first round upset of the 18-year-old No. 1 French junior, Paul Barrelet de Ricou, Luddy caused me to be toasted by the maitre d' and the entire staff of Maxim's - mighty heady stuff to a young traveler.

Mishu had drawn Bill Tilden in the first round at St. Cloud, where the French Championships were then played and, though hopelessly overmatched, he resolved to leave his mark. I was in the front row of the stadium directly in back of Nicolai, preparing to drink in every shot of the match, as I would do with all the others. At the conclusion of the warm-up, the umpire said "Play," whereupon Nicolai, who had won the toss, turned his back to the net and Tilden and started to converse with the center service linesman. Bill, who could stand anything but being upstaged, put his hands on his hips and turned to the gallery at his end as if to say, "What does this donkey think he's doing?" Nicolai, without a glance over his shoulder threw up the ball and hit it backwards into the service box where it went past Bill on the second bounce. Tilden turned in astonishment to observe Mishu now claiming the first point and preparing a serve to the ad court. Tilden was outraged, but Nicolai, protesting mostly with both hands, insisted that he often served backwards and since play had been called and he had served an ace the score was 15-0.

Several years later in the first round of Wimbledon doubles, Nicolai and Luddy were drawn against Berkeley Bell and Greg Mangin, a high-seeded American team. Mrs. Fitz Eugene Dixon, whose husband was that year's non-playing U.S. Davis Cup team captain and whose son, Fitz Jr., once owned the Philadelphia 76ers basketball franchise plus another asset or two, must have picked up the wrong dossier on Count Salm, for she offered Berk and Greg ten bucks for each time they could wing either member of Luddy's team. The Americans had never even met their opponents and probably assumed that the normally warm and friendly Mrs. Dixon had the goods on them. Also, a sawbuck then was a mighty nice supplement to the not-so-adequate Davis Cup subsistence allowance (it was "amateur" only in those days).

Upon hearing of the plot, I had no compunction about passing on the word to my pals - it's a different game of stud when you know where the aces are. On hearing the news, they guffawed and began dodging imaginary balls. Being fairly wily European types, Nicolai and Luddy decided they would try to trump this trick. I had finished a doubles match soon after they had started and came over in time to see Mangin clobber an easy lob a mile out, but close to Mishu who had stepped inside the baseline to offer a more tempting target. It didn't take long to fathom "my team's" strategy. With shortish lobs and even softer serves than usual, they would tempt Berk and Greg into risking a ten-spot hit at every potential opportunity. As I looked on, the errors piled up for Bell and Mangin who, as all tennis players are well aware can happen, began to "get the elbow" as their concentration went down the drain. It would have been poetic justice if Nicolai and Luddy had pulled off a big upset, but the close score did earn them new respect among their peers and probably a few useful seeded spots in some less-than-major tournaments.

When the Nazis overran Austria, they sought to utilize Count Salm's close ties with the British and Americans for espionage purposes. The SS had unearthed the damning evidence that there was Semitic heritage on a branch of the Von Hoogsträten family tree, and their method for Luddy's impressment was blackmail. He would be imprisoned as a criminal-by-blood if he refused to serve the master race as a titled spy.

On the morning of his anticipated acceptance, with the SS forcing the door of his Vienna apartment, Luddy opened a window and dove to his death. Luddy's American father-in-law, H.H. Rogers, not only violently disapproved of his daughter's marriage but also reportedly used his considerable parental and financial influence to break it up (such things were not so uncommon in that era). It is said by one close to the family that Luddy's letters to his bride, and her's to him, were intercepted and that both of them may have gone to their graves believing the other did not care. Their only child, Peter Salm, grew up without the privilege of ever seeing a father he could not have failed to be proud of. I later had the opportunity of being perhaps the first to tell Peter of the everywhere-respected and popular man his father had been – especially with me. Peter himself had a son and for reasons that are pleasant to contemplate, named him Ludwig.

CHAPTER NINETEEN

Days of Grace

WAY BACK IN THE LATE 1950S, MY GOOD FRIENDS Malcolm and Carolyn Reybold asked me to join them and their Manhattan neighbor Grace Kelly (whose father did the building's brickwork) for the annual moose, elk or other large ruminant's steak dinner at Rothmann's Steakhouse. Being unattached at the time, I accepted with alacrity.

Grace's acting career had just gotten underway with some TV roles, but even then she had a tendency to imbibe a bit more than enough. She'd been to a cocktail party before we headed for Long Island, and, apart from looking, to put it politely, quite disheveled, she was somewhat argumentative. End of "romance!"

A year later, another call came from Malcolm, telling me that Grace, whose career had enjoyed a meteoric rise, was totally on the wagon, and asked if I was game for a second Rothmann's try? He added that she would like to make up for last year.

With a snowstorm predicted, I brought along a shovel, and off we went in Malcolm's new Buick. This time Grace looked every bit the stunner that she sure was, and all went well. In fact, well enough for me to leave my snow shovel as kind of a fraternity pin in her foyer when I saw her home.

Grace Kelly

We'd already made a date for dinner the next night, then another, and another.

The Reybolds, particularly Carolyn, who was later Grace's maid of honor in her Monte Carlo royal wedding to Prince Rainier, were elated with their matchmaking luck. Show-people friends Grace met with me included Ed Sullivan, swash-buckling actor Tyrone Power and Gary Cooper, with whom she later co-starred in *High Noon*. We'd also get together with Grace's brother, John, and his nifty Miss America friend, whose name escapes me.

Much as you may delight in someone's company, it's tough to fall in love with a girl who just can't help playing a role. One time, Grace put on a tape of multiple animal sounds (even whales!) and one by one proceeded to act out each as I fell asleep on the carpet. She lived in a kind of a fairy tale princess world, which she would ultimately occupy in real-ity. Grace was a huge box office success, and in my book, a superb actress.

A no longer non-mentionable item: one day at my hobby-born Sutton Place, Town Tennis Club, Oleg Cassini remark-ably asked if I would tell him when (and if) I was no longer seeing Grace. I told him we'd been secretly married for weeks. Shortly thereafter, a near daily delivery of a dozen long-stem roses began arriving at Grace's apartment, sans any card. Knowing Oleg pretty well, I correctly guessed that he was the mystery sender. I'd bring some of the roses to my delighted office staff, others we'd send to the Reybolds and other friends. Heartfelt thanks, Oleg! Though Oleg's was not exactly my style of approach, to each his own. In time, it worked well enough for Oleg (his florist as well) to become a serious suitor for quite a spell.

Curtain call: alas our "brief encounter" was not destined to survive our disparate lifestyles, and one morning a taxi delivered the snow shovel to my office. The dramatic finale was so typical of Grace. That "inevitable sadness," I couldn't help guffawing until my staff thought I'd lost my marbles. I wrote a nice thank-you note.

Althea Gibson

CHAPTER TWENTY

The Case of Althea Gibson

WHEN ALTHEA GIBSON HAD BECOME A CHAMPION-ship-mettle competitor in 1950, five all-white top 10 tennis players: Frank Shields, Don McNeill, Cliff Sutter, Gil Hall and I, whom I'd finally "persuaded" the U.S. Lawn Tennis Association to appoint to its 25-member executive committee, could not believe their ears on hearing an almost whispered motion proposed to bar Althea from the upcoming U.S. Nationals at Forest Hills and prevent her from becoming the first black player to compete at the highest level of American tennis.

There had been no prior discussion of any such idea, at least not for us to know of, but at the far end of the long luncheon table at the Vanderbilt Hotel (then the official USLTA hostelry) there had been a star chamber get-together sustained by the customary double Manhattan aperitifs, and although it seems inconceivable that any presumably mature Association fathers could be hatching this dumb plot, there was no question as to their intent. I am constrained to add that Russell Kingman, the USLTA president, was abroad at the time, and I can't dismiss the suspicion that the meeting was timed to precede his return and certain veto. Russell was one of the rare breed of truly altruistic sports executives, also a booster for my own and other progressive help-the-game ideas.

Up to that time, none of our five guys had reason to qualify as minority activists, but we admired as well as liked Althea, and our sense of fair play was rudely affronted. In honesty, perhaps it was not entirely the bald inequity of the case, but righteous indignation at being railroaded by the badge-wearer fraternity that caused me to jump up and ask how they could be unaware of the recently enacted State anti-bias law – and to warn them that they could expect to read their names in every sports-page headline. Their absurdly naïve legal stance was that being a member of a USLTA sectional association was a prerequisite to competing in the Nationals! As has been forever typical of ladder-rung advances in sports officialdom, any opinions of mere athletes are rarely heeded. This could explain why I have seldom been the ruling party's favorite player.

That September from the northwest sidewall of the stadium at Forest Hills, Shields, McNeill, Hall and I had one eye on the stadium match and the other on Althea playing Louise Brough on the adjoining grandstand court. While few players like to see the No. 2 seed lose, and especially Louise, we were stirred when Althea came within two points of a huge upset.

Gibson not only broke the color barrier at the U.S. Championships that year, but went on, of course, to win two women's singles titles at Forest Hills as well as two at Wimbledon and another in France at Roland Garros. She could afford a laugh at the outrageous act of bigotry that had been considered. But as novelist James Baldwin cried out, "To be a Negro in this country and constantly be made aware of it is to be in a rage most of your life."

In 1990, 32 years after her second victory at Wimbledon and the U.S. Nationals, I found myself sitting next to her in the Royal Box at Wimbledon watching the final. Life goes on.

CHAPTER TWENTY ONE

Tennis with Bobby Fischer

FOR THOSE WHO MAY RECALL AND HAVE WONDERED about the unfathomable antics of the super-cerebral Bobby Fischer, king of kings of the chessboard, my experience of an afternoon with Bobby should be either enlightening or further puzzling.

As an average "patzer" chess player (the term is familiar to other patzers), I was a consumer of *The New York Times* chess column, written by my friend the late Al Horowitz, a former national champion. A week prior to Fischer's 1974 trip to Iceland for his world championship match with Russia's Boris Spassky, Al phoned me to ask if, of all things, I would play some tennis with Bobby. Of course I said yes.

The next day, all in whites, Bobby came by my hobby-born, rooftop Town Tennis Club on Sutton Place with Rosser Reeves, a generous contributor to chess causes and the 1966 retired head of the big-three Ted Bates ad agency.

Also accompanying Bobby was a medium-young, medium-blond lady whose name failed to register, perhaps because Bobby kept asking her to tell it to him again; indications were that Bobby did not live by chess alone.

I had heard that Bobby rarely ventured more than an arm's length from a chessboard, and to my surprise, he hit the tennis ball vehemently and with good coordination. He was only mildly overweight and not at all tired from the workout. When I asked him what he would like to drink he asked for an orange juice, milk and a beer – all at the same time. We sat around for awhile and I cautiously volunteered the idea that Bobby might want to meet Mark McCormack, with whom I had put together a 600-outlet Arnold Palmer Cleaning Center franchise.

I had been warned that Bobby was suspicious of everybody except his mother, and my overture was proffered in low key. Even so, though a breakfast meeting was set up with Mark who flew in from Cleveland, Bobby could not bring himself to attend.

The Fisher-Spassky match was receiving tremendous front-page publicity because it had become blown up as a contest

Bobby Fischer

between U.S. brainpower and Russia's. The championship was to be decided by the first winner of 12 of the 23 game points won (one point for a win, a half point for a draw). When I pointed out to Bobby that he would easily be the most famous person in the world for 23 days, he tilted his head a little and with a pixie-like grin asked me how did I know it wouldn't be 12 days – as many as it would take for him to win without losing or drawing a game!

On the basis of that afternoon's enjoyable association, there was no hint of the unpredictable side to Bobby's makeup, and I would have rated him as self-assured but not abrasively so, engagingly friendly, humorous and as well-adjusted as his stratospheric IQ would permit.

The Shah of Iran

CHAPTER TWENTY TWO

The Shah and I

THIS CONCERNS A RARE EXPERIENCE IN WHICH A SHARED belief in something much out of the ordinary welded a special bond between me and the Shah of Iran.

In November of 1952, my office switchboard announced a call from a "secretary of His Imperial Majesty, Shah of Iran." I had partnered the Shah in a State Department-arranged doubles game at New York's River Club two days before, and I took the call prepared to deal with some waggish friend who had heard about it. But a formally accented lady's voice asked if I were Mr. Sidney B. Wood, Jr., to which I may have replied, "No, this is Tutankhamen." However, there was enough note of concern in the clipped British accent on the other end to make the call reasonably credible. So I apologized and was more than surprised to hear myself invited to join my potentate partner for Thanksgiving dinner at the Waldorf and to be told that there would be just four of us. In the interest of maintaining our nation's public relations posture, such an invite should not be regretted. I then told the secretary that, literally minutes before, I had dictated a note to the Shah telling him what a pleasant experience it had been playing with him and what a surprisingly able and unstuffy partner he had been.

In the locker room, before going out on the court for the

encounter, I had been earnestly briefed by a U.S. protocol gentleman as to how I was to address my exalted sidekick. To those who play a bit of doubles, you know that it could be a cumbersome exercise if you must precede such split-second injunctions as "yours" and "mine" by shouting, "Your Imperial Majesty." But almost instantly on meeting my partner, this was clearly not to be a problem. I said, "I am, of course, Sidney. What do you prefer to be called?" He said, with a wide smile, "I am, of course, Reza."

I had a torn shoulder tendon, so Reza had to serve for me, but we combined well enough to perform credibly against Stanley Rumbough and Henry Breck – two much better than club type players – who didn't hesitate to boom His Majesty whenever they got him in their sights.

At the Thanksgiving dinner, Reza's other guests were two dazzling daughters of the Brazilian ambassador and Grover Whalen, Manhattan's perennial host to visiting notables, who arrived during dessert. We then proceeded to the limousines for our trip to a performance of the smash musical South Pacific. And what a trip! For the entire distance from Lexington to Eighth Avenue the 42nd Street traffic was held at bay while our siren-screeching entourage swept by – all the way on the wrong side of the two-way street. Soon after we were seated, a buddy of mine, Henry Cole, waved and started toward me along our row to say hello. To his astonishment and mine, a burly Secret Service lady arose at least five seats away and blocked him off. My evening was made.

After the show, we returned to Reza's Waldorf Towers apartment where a number of the show's cast members and a few dozen other guests had assembled before going downstairs to a midnight supper party. Reza was being lionized, but, after some moments, I saw him beckoning from across the room for me to follow him into a sitting room where he locked the door against intruders. Then ensued a remarkable conversation which I shall repeat as faithfully as can be recalled. He asked whether I had really written that note just before his secretary called. When I emphatically replied, "Yes," he said, "I felt at that instant you were trying to get in touch with me." He continued, "You know we Iranians have strong faith in such perceptions." He asked me if I, by chance, shared these convictions, and I told him that not only did I believe in such phenomena but that I had undergone a number of dramatically convincing experiences of this nature in my own life. We talked briefly about this and other things, and as we shook hands he asked if I would later fly to Teheran for a visit. Being involved at home with a number of demanding matters I failed to follow up what would surely have been an enviable and lifetime rewarding experience, and this is something I have always regretted.

We proceeded to supper in the Waldorf's Peacock Alley Room at a single long table. Mary Martin, the superb star of *South Pacific,* was on Reza's right and I, surprisingly, was seated on his left. Reza, whose interest in tennis verged on intense, asked a number of questions of the same variety I often receive. At one point, I was describing a comical incident during a French mixed doubles championship final with the incomparable Helen Wills Moody as my partner at Stade Roland Garros in Paris (with two double Courvoisiers under my belt). Reza and Mary Martin were listening closely, but all at once, I realized the entire table of some 30 guests had stopped their conversation and, in deference to the Shah, had become my audience. There was no retreat, but fortunately, the punch line went across well enough to earn a favorable score on the laugh meter.

The image of the Shah of Iran as portrayed in the news media of later years bears little resemblance to the qualities I found in him. Media? That should evoke thoughts of land where the Medes and the Persians roamed. To me, Reza was completely unpretentious, impulsively warm and an amusing companion who could be as serious or lighthearted as the occasion warranted.

On the tennis court, where one's character is often laid bare, he proved to be a partner who needed no indulgence, followed directions with appreciation and attention, who played with zest and was the epitome of sportsmanship. In short, if you hadn't a clue that Reza Shah Pahlevi was indeed master of the fates of some 35 million Persian souls, you would much look forward to having him for a friend.

The Shah's abdication from power and shameful abandonment by the pusillanimous Carter administration recalls David Frost's sober reminder following Jack Kennedy's tragic murder. "No matter how high the throne upon which we sit, our tails still touch the ground."

Reza is gone – could it have been Allah's merciful purpose to shield him from helplessly witnessing the yet continuing degradation of his beloved nation? Some years later, entirely by coincidence, Reza's nephew rented what we call our "big house" in Southampton for the summer, and even at that point there was some shadowy concern about Khomeni's assassins learning of his whereabouts. In 1995, we became friends with Reza's brother and his wife who wintered in Palm Beach. The chemistry was ready-made.

CHAPTER TWENTY THREE

The First US Open
Box Seats

IN THE POST-WORLD WAR I ERA, WITH HEADLINER stadium-fillers such as Ellsworth Vines, Don Budge, Fred Perry and Bobby Riggs moving on to successively join the pay-for-play circuit, amateur tennis fell deeper into the depths of spectator disinterest year after year. Our National Championship, the modern-day US Open, was played at an initially overflowing Forest Hills stadium (during the era of Bill Tilden, Bill Johnston, Vincent Richards, Rene Lacoste, Henri Cochet and Jean Borotra), but as public interest declined, blocks of tickets were handed out to such as the Boy Scouts and YMCA to add a few bodies to the embarrassingly thin spectator presence. The U.S. Lawn Tennis Association was so impoverished that its Davis Cup captains were named not for their tennis savvy but because they could pay their own way!

In the 1940s, I got the idea of fitting 22 eight-seat boxes against the 14-foot stadium interior west wall in the stadium of Forest Hills to bring in some higher price, high profile spectators. In a typical official reaction to any new idea, my untraditional stadium presentation was zapped – that is, until I offered to bank the installation, to be reimbursed from box sales. Guess what. In a single morning, I had no problem selling all 176 seats to corporate and other tennis-booster friends for a net pickup of a more-than-welcome three grand. The entire 12,000-seat stadium, sparsely attended, even for the weekend finals, cleared, I believe, less than $15,000.

CHAPTER TWENTY FOUR

Supreme Court

SUPREME COURT, A TRANSPORTABLE CUSHIONED surface idea I came up with, was originally a help-the-game concept for pal Mike Davies, whom oil and sports tycoon Lamar Hunt had recruited to run his World Championship Tennis (WCT) indoor pro tour. A that point, nothing yet had proven feasible and Lamar's bold world-wide indoor arena play dream was about to become a nightmare. Supreme Court was far from perfect but for more than a couple of decades it has been the workhorse surface for virtually every worldwide indoor pro event.

It didn't start off without its problems, however. After I patented "Supreme Court" and went through many trial and error workouts, it debuted in the late 1960s at a whistle-stop event at the Montreal Forum. The competing players were Rod Laver, Ken Rosewall, Pancho Gonzales, Roy Emerson, Fred Stolle, Pancho Segura, Dennis Ralston and Pierre Barthes, with the promoter and manager of the tour being a fellow named Wally Dill. An hour or so before the evening's first match, most of the aforementioned legends were sitting courtside, cackling for me to hurry up and stripe the lines so they could try out this new strange court surface. In the rush of things, the measurement diagram had been mislaid and I

wasn't sure where the service line belonged. Advice was shout-
ed from the bench with most of the boys insisting it had to
be at the mid-point – which I knew to be wrong. To quiet the
experts – especially Gonzales who was never wrong – I asked
him to try a couple of serves. When he couldn't put them in
within the tape where he wanted it, we changed it to where it
should be – 21 feet from the net.

Stolle led off against Rosewall that night and while running
wide for a forehand, he stopped hard, sundering my experi-
mental seam tape, and slid under the carpet up to his chest.
Fred, who is not without humor, remained prone and leaning
on one elbow and beckoned me to come over. It was too late
for a sneak exit, so I pulled Fred to his feet and, amid catcalls
from the spectators, used a staple gun to secure the selvages to
the pallet below.

The next night, while I was safely at dinner on Long Island,
a call came from Dill, who asked me if I was sitting down.
"Have you seen four baselines on one court?" he asked. The
night before, there wasn't time to tape the alley lines to the
court (there was no doubles that night), so on the arena aisle,
I had chalked a diagram for the young executive from Mon-
santo (an early associate in court development) to complete
the following morning. But fate and the arena mop crew in-
tervened, and by morning my layout was no more. Mr. Mon-
santo, who shall remain anonymous, was clearly no tennis
maven. He remembered the 4 ¹/₂ foot spacing between lines...
but which lines? You'd think he might have asked!

CHAPTER TWENTY FIVE

Once I Was Gross
at Roland Garros

AT THE AGE OF 13, I WAS SO SKINNY THAT OF ALL THE
young hopefuls at the Berkeley Tennis Club in California, I
was the only one who could stick his hand through the hole of
the tennis ball discard box and squeeze out the most luscious
of the slightly-used spheres. Although the box was a repository for donations to the YMCA and other worthy causes, I
recall having no qualms about providing for myself and my
fellow teeners.

My clear conscience may have been the result of long unre-
quited services as ball boy to the lady world champion, Helen
Wills, later Helen Wills Moody. "Queen Helen," a media title
that her unbroken string of victories well merited, never had
to worry where her next tennis ball was coming from, and it
never dawned on her how desperately I coveted even one out
of the half dozen that she would use for every practice session.
The discards were always good enough to have their Spalding
or Wilson names still visible on the felt, and to any sub-junior
who has played a lot of sets with only the rubber undercover
remaining, they were precious pearls.

Six years later as the previous year's Wimbledon winner, in
one of those stranger-than-fiction tales, I found myself as Hel-
en's requested mixed doubles partner for the French Cham-

pionships in Paris. Alas, however, for "reasons beyond my control," our French title victory was denied by Napoleon... Napoleon brandy, that is.

The afternoon of our mixed final, I first had to meet the rock-steady René Lacoste in singles, losing to him in an unreal five-and-a-quarter-hour, five-set grueller on a searing, 98-degree afternoon (one of the longest matches ever played in fact). Afterwards, we were laid out on adjoining locker room tables, and in seconds the cramps were jumping all over us.

Hellen Wills Moody with Wood

They hit me everywhere, the worst of my life. As René and I writhed and groaned, Fred Moody, Helen's husband, appeared with a pair of double Courvoisiers, Fred's remedy for many ailments. He carefully trickled one down my throat, but René, an abstemious Prometheus to the end, turned his down, and Fred dosed me with that one, also.

Then, in walks Pierre Gillou, the tournament's referee and head of everything tennis in France, all hands and shrugs, to announce that despite his minutes' earlier assurance (before my brandy medication) that the mixed doubles final had been rescheduled for the next day, it was now to be played immediately. Queen Helen, at that point in her life, was the most self-centered of champions imaginable, as well as being every tournament's prime meal ticket whose every wish was a royal command. In America, she was evey bit as famous as Babe Ruth or Jack Dempsey, and internationally more so. Possibly Helen was unaware that René and I had barely made it off the court on our own legs (and certainly of my brandy-benumbed condition). In any case, Gillou said she flatly refused to play the ladies' singles and mixed finals on the same, next day for fear of being overtired before Wimbledon's opening day, two weeks later, and Gillou capitulated.

After five humidity-draining sets, you have no idea how even a short snort can hit you, and I was now feeling no pain and ready to joust with Bill Tilden, Henri Cochet and Fred Perry, all at the same time. So, with no one around with enough sense or initiative to restrain me from doing something idiotic, I told Gillou I'd be on the court in minutes. I then headed for the locker room and, as I was struggling into my long gabardines, I conceived the brilliant idea of inserting two Dunlop tire ashtrays under my belt to support my undulating midriff muscles.

Thus accoutered, I descended to the pit where Fred Perry and Betty Nuthall were our intended victims. Also on hand was a stadium-packed gallery (the bleachers were always jammed for Helen). At net, rallying with Betty, I was not encouraged to see more than one ball coming at me at the same time, and it seemed best to select one to hit and let the others pass. Knowing me as a serious competitor, Betty no doubt assumed that I was clowning a bit – for which I was also known. But my pal Perry, who couldn't believe I was still standing after my marathon, came up to net to ask if I were okay. I said, "I'm smashed," and retreated to the baseline to try a few serves.

My muscles were no less done in, only anesthetized by Mr. Moody's two double shots, and when I tried to toss up one of the three balls, it wouldn't come loose. The ball stuck in my fingers and I could not put up a toss to hit a serve. We had won the toss and I told Helen she would have to serve first, and it was 0-3 when I finally had to step up and serve. Amazingly, the ball left my hand, made contact with my racquet and actually landed in its intended service box. Heading for net, I felt a little bump on my shoe and observed one of the ashtrays that had dislodged itself, dropped down my trousers and was rolling along with me. Play was called by the umpire to remove the alien object. To my best recollection, some contact was made with the shots that came my way, but in a very short time we lost the match.

The inexcusably stupid part of my gaff was that even at age 20, with no real idea of what too much liquor could do to my coordination, something should have warned me on my own before my getting out on the court – certainly when I was seeing double – that I should get the hell out of there, no matter the consequences.

CHAPTER TWENTY SIX

Frequent Flier

"Had I known, I'd rather have had birds than airplanes."
- Charles A. Lindberg.

As LATE AS 1941, THE FOURTEEN-SEATERS OF LOCKHEED'S
and Ford's Tri-motor were the only commercial airplanes
around, and all seats came with ammonia capsules and sick-
bags. The airlines advertised New York to Los Angeles or San
Francisco in 28 ³/₄ hours, compared with the 84 hours (three
days and four nights) by train on Santa Fe's Super Chief. I was
eventually presented with an impressive 100,000 Mile Club
plaque by American Airlines, though I may have travelled half
that distance with them. But, never did we make it coast-to-
coast in less than 40 hours. All those of us crazy enough to
keep coming back for more had an overlong acquaintance
with the wooden benches at Denver and Salt Lake City, waiting for breaks in the mountain ranges' weather. Practically
every time I'd land, I'd swear that was the last trip, but like
coming out of the hospital, in a week or two you forget how
much it hurt. Hoping to save two days, you would decide to
fly "once more."

My most frequent fellow flyer was Roger Pryor, who understandably didn't relish unnecessary hours apart from his

nifty actress wife, Ann Sothern. In those early airborne days it would be a close call to judge who was the nuttiest, the pioneer heads of airlines or guys like Roger and me who helped to pay the early-day freight.

Roger and I would phone each other to check our flight plans, meet at Newark or Burbank (the only extant airports), shake our heads and board up for another who-knew-what -kind-of-trip.

To those nowadays air travelers who may occasionally complain of a rough trip, I offer the following: My maiden voyage, at age 19, was when my train trip to the Pacific Southwest Tournament in Los Angeles was derailed in Kansas City. The conductor told me we would be in the station for a half hour, so I made a quick call to a Kansas player friend, Junior Coen, and bought some magazines. After meandering back to the gate, I was startled to see the lights of our observation platform heading west, not only with my six racquets and bags, but with a newly-met, dazzling starlet en route to Hollywood. I raced back to the phone and somehow talked a barnstorming-type, probably broke, pilot into chasing after the Super Chief. Of a lot of bumpy rides I later had in those days, this was the worst. We flew perhaps 200 feet above the Santa Fe tracks in the hot sun, and when we passed over the numerous corrugated-roof buildings at rail-side, the little plane would pitch up and down like a kite, and yaw wildly in the thermals.

A couple of hours later, we caught sight of the train and it looked like we could beat it to Herrington, Kansas in time. Herrington had no airport, but my dauntless pilot headed for any clear area he could find. In due course, we spied the station and a mile or two away we swooped down onto a fallow field and taxied up to an astonished farmer. Our host immediately entered into the spirit of the chase and led us to his barn where he had a nicely preserved Model T which he cranked up, and we tore at a mad 50 mph to the station with only minutes to spare before the train got there. My bags and racquets were still aboard, as was my disbelieving fair maiden friend.

CHAPTER TWENTY SEVEN

Near Miss

JOHN HAY "JOCK" WHITNEY WAS A FRIEND AND THE controlling shareholder of Freeport Texas Sulphur, as well as a substantial backer of Dave Selznick's *Gone With the Wind*.

Jock had been helpful to me in our California sulphur operation, and one time we decided we could combine a business meeting with a flight back to New York. Our plane made a stopover in the dark at Albuquerque's then-minuscule airport, and we were told it wouldn't leave for a half hour. So we wandered to the end of the runway and coming back were dismayed to see our trip to New York taxiing for a takeoff. Jock had a slightly lame leg, but I took off like a rabbit for the "office." Among other things, I told its manager that Jock's cousin, Sonny, was chairman of Pan Am, and he grudgingly phoned the plane to return (they had simply neglected to count people before leaving). We were stony-faced by the other passengers when we boarded – taking off and landing in those days was often a nauseating experience, due to the five minutes or so of real bumping as well as the noxious fumes from the exhaust.

CHAPTER TWENTY EIGHT

Deputy Wood

I GUESS YOU CAN SAY THAT THE MINING BUSINESS IS NOT for the faint of heart.

One morning our sulphur operations manager Lefty Wright arrived at our Beverly Hills office with the shocking news that three of our hands at the mine had: a) blown up the powder magazines, b) dumped one of our loaded 18-wheel trucks over a precipice, c) terrorized our 40-man camp, nearly killing one of our shift foremen and badly beating another. Lefty had gotten the word late the night before when he was at Big Pine, the mine's 60-miles-distance nearest habitation, and he immediately headed south to us.

What to do? All day I tried, to no avail, to reach the county sheriff in Independence, 25 miles south of Big Pine, where the strikers were believed to be, so, acting more out of rage than reason, I sent Lefty and our office manager Eddie Burns, Sr. to pick up two shotguns and get the barrels cut down. By late afternoon, joined by Ed Jr. (the Burnses had once won a U.S. Father and Son tennis championships), we headed the 300 miles north for Big Pine. At that point, I wasn't scared, just enraged and bent on justice.

Around midnight, we were at the Sheriff's house, but his toughest assignments were usually handling drunks or brawls.

After much palavering, he copped out, made us deputies and handed us his only two pairs of handcuffs. In those days in the sparsely settled Owens Valley, there were no such things as state troopers or other law enforcement people.

We then drove the 60 miles to the mine without incident and found things in an even worse shambles than Lefty had heard. As dawn was breaking, we held a camp meeting to get the full facts, and though many of the men volunteered to help us run down the so-called strikers, we assured them we would take care of matters. The six vehicles in camp had been stripped of distributors, but we piled some of the miners with families into the pickup to drop off at Big Pine.

One of the culprits had taken our mine pickup for his use and, perhaps not caring to face murder charges, had dropped our two seriously injured men at Bishop's Hospital, 16 miles north of Big Pine.

By early morning, we arrived there and saw how brutally our two men had been beaten. Ray Palmer had a pickaxe hole in his head and he would never be the same. We were further incensed but more sobered by the need for immediately dealing with the crisis. Again, I argued at length with the Sheriff to at least be with us to make the arrests, but his devotion to duty was not nearly strong enough to move him. Although the realities of the situation grew on me, I could not picture us just picking up the broken pieces and starting up again with no retribution for the crippling vandalism, but especially for the brutality of the attackers. So we just had to go through with things, whatever the risks.

It didn't take long for Lefty to learn that our quarry was holed up in a four-cabin motel near Big Pine, though God knows why they were still hanging around. If it was a strike, all of the rest of our crew opposed it. We paid the best wages and put out the best chow of any mine in California, so what other motive could these guys have except just looking for a pretty grim kind of adventure?

We knew which one was our target cabin and, around midnight, we pulled up a couple of hundred yards away with lights out. I wasn't scared, just petrified. Betting there would be no gun-in-hand lookout waiting for us on his cot, Eddie Jr. was to cut through a window screen through which "Field Marshal Wood" would break into the room, with Eddie Jr. beaming two big flashlights so I could see to unbolt the door for Eddie Sr. and Lefty.

It was a flawless plan except...Eddie Jr. failed to cut the screen quite down to the sill and I crash-landed on the floor. Hearing the screams, Eddie Sr. and Lefty kicked through the log door (why hadn't we just done that to start with?), gun-whipped the third occupant who was there, and, with pipe and gun barrels, quickly stilled some frenzied resistance. We put handcuffs on two of the guys, taped up the third and wrapped them tight in their bloodied sheets.

Lefty brought the pickup to the door and we drove to the Sheriff's house in Independence. After considerable 1:00 AM door-knocking, his head popped out of an upstairs window. He offered a "fine work, boys" and pleaded with us to drop our cargo over the county line. Though much tempted to leave them on his doorstep, we accepted and drove over the county line, dumping the three into a roadside ditch. Crazily, we never could learn anything about what happened to them. But it developed that one was a Folsom Prison escapee, another was on parole, and the third was probably just another loser joining up.

Two days later when I got back to Beverly Hills, I was so worked up over the harm any of these guys might do to my wife and baby son that by the very next day we rented a new house.

CHAPTER TWENTY NINE

The Hotfoot

THE SULPHUR BUSINESS DIDN'T GIVE ME BACK ALL I put into it, especially my foot.

One night, while working at the mine with only car lights and carbide hat lamps, I stumbled on an overlapping plank which served as our walkway across an 84-inch deep curing vat of molten sulphur and went overboard.

I would have gotten away with a bruise or two, but we had just made a test run and there were four inches of the molten sulphur on the bottom – its melting point is 285 degrees Fahrenheit. Somehow I was able to claw onto the 2" by 12" plank and only my right foot went into the soup. Lefty Wright and a tennis buddy, Harold Blauer, who was working for me at the time, grabbed my wrists and pulled me up before I was a goner.

The mine had only aspirin and a Band-Aid type kit, so with the nearest real hospital in Los Angeles, they threw a mattress and barrel of ice into a pickup and we made the 360-mile midnight ride with Harold and Lefty holding me down.

The foot was saved with some fancy grafting, but I had to wire the U.S. Davis Cup Committee to count me out for that summer's play.

CHAPTER THIRTY

"Nuts to you, Mrs. Astor"

ALMOST EVERY YEAR, IN THE BYGONE DAYS OF amateur tennis camaraderie, a lucky newcomer to the tournament scene would be earmarked for special indoctrination through a tacit understanding among more seasoned citizens of the circuit. One such new arrival was Tamio Abe, Japan's upcoming new star, whose game was clearly superior to his command of English.

To help Tami better communicate his menu requirements we (yes, I too was on the "education committee") explained how he should place his mealtime orders. At the Wilmington Country Club in Delaware, the earliest grass court stop on our schedule, Tami was instructed that for breakfast, "Will you spend the weekend with me?" would get him two poached eggs on toast with bacon and, "You jump in the lake" would take care of his tea with lemon. The next morning, none of us showed up until Tami had finished his meal, and he was somewhat reflective during the day. For some time thereafter he would wait for his friends before entering the dining room.

To assure Mr. Abe's social acceptance at Newport later in the summer, he was carefully groomed in certain amenities. For instance at Mrs. Vincent (Helen) Astor's annual lunch for the players, when Tami was introduced, he bowed impeccably to his hostess and in near perfect accents said, "Nuts to you, Mrs. Astor," a Broadway *bon mot* then going the rounds. Helen and I were playing together in the member-guest mixed doubles that week, which we lucked out, and I had the opportunity to thank her for her typical graciousness in having seated Tami to her right. As a pleasing aside, I would comment that the name of Astor was no detriment to one's social invitation list, and "my partner" as I would thereafter introduce as Helen, never failed me at a benefit or other occasion I would ask her to. At one, I seated her at a banquette between Jack Dempsey and Babe Ruth, and she could not be dislodged. Helen was unequivocally the grand dame of New York's somewhat amorphous social scene, but she took it far less earnestly than those in-waiting.

We were never really mean to Tami or any of his fellow tour freshmen, and he was obviously delighted with the attention he was accorded. The same such things may still go on, but, with coaches, agents, psychologists and trips to the banks, there can't be much time at today's tournaments for non-profit horseplay.

After the eastern summer tournament circuit ended, Tami visited our family in Pasadena, and Frederic Chopin must have turned over more than once as we two-piano dueted some of his faster and louder preludes that were never meant for more than one player (piano player that is). Tami stayed with us two or three weeks during which he kept buying new shirts and silk socks, disdaining the local laundry and discarding what he had worn. Clever these Japanese? During his stay he got even with me for whatever I had done to him in the past by cleaning my clock in the final at the Midwick Tournament after I'd put out the cannonading Ellsworth Vines in the semifinals.

CHAPTER THIRTY ONE

Practice Imperfect

FOR REASONS THAT MYSTIFIED ME FOR YEARS, NO matter how earnestly I tried to beat out practice opponents, I have simply never been able to perform at peak ability in practice or exhibition matches.

The first absolute convincer was in the season of 1932 when Greg Mangin, twice the champ at the U.S. Indoors and a heck of a net rusher, and I were named as the International Club's team of two to play Davis Cup format matches in Europe against England, France, Germany and Australia. Greg and I practiced with each other at least five days a week. Although I would bust my britches every time to beat him, I never, never could end up a session ahead in sets. Meanwhile, I was winning my matches against the opposing countries' best players in our series while Greg was not. Yet I continued to end up not ever better than even in our practice sets.

And then came the time when the tournament draws brought us against each other. The first was in the fourth round of Wimbledon in 1932, where, amazingly, I knocked off Greg in three straight sets. The next was in the final of the Irish Championships in Dublin where I won in five sets, and the next two were back-to-back finals in the States where I beat him in successive finals (Seabright, N.J. in four sets and Southampton,

N.Y. in five). Even between these events – we were probably equally curious to see what would occur in practice – I still could never end up better than splitting sets.

At least three other major tournament winners, Vic Seixas, Ted Schroeder and Bob Falkenburg, were also lousy practice players, and about all we have ever surmised was that no matter how hard we tried to concentrate, we somehow couldn't resist experimenting with some new shot, something that would never occur in match play, in which even a single unfocused point is a potential threat to your year's ranking.

A happy Wood with Greg Mangin

Jean Borotra

CHAPTER THIRTY TWO

The Double-Hit That Cost Jean Borotra the 1927 Wimbledon Title

JEAN BOROTRA, ONE OF FRANCE'S MULTIPLE-WINNING Davis Cup "Four Musketeers," is on record as having garnered two Wimbledon men's singles titles. But had the umpire found the courage to immediately make the right call on a match-point, a double hit by fellow Musketeer Henri Cochet in the 1927 Wimbledon final, Jean would have owned his third win.

It was my first visit to Wimbledon (I lost in the first round to René Lacoste) and I'd managed my way into a first row center seat behind the umpire's stand for the final, where from about twenty feet, I could see and hear everything that went on during the court changes. I've never really been fraternally comfortable about relating the unsportsmanlike hard facts of a quite incredible experience. But when my friend Alan Little, who has made Wimbledon's matchless library our game's one-of-a-kind repository for every tennis book and major magazine published, exhumed for me the name of Ashley Tinnen, the match's umpire, from his musty archives, I decided the story should not be omitted from this compilation.

In a rapid-fire volleying exchange at 5-4 and match point in the fifth set for Borotra, Cochet's racquet made an audible frame-contact, followed by a stabbed touch of the ball for a mis-hit "winner." I witnessed and clearly heard the double-

115

hit, but possibly it was not that obvious to the non-player press corps seated at courtside but further from the net. Then, instead of an immediate "game, set and match, Borotra" announcement, with Jean waiting expectantly for his Cup teammate to congratulate him, there ensued an embarrassed momentary pause until in these still remembered, exact words from Tinnen, "Monsieur Cochet, did you perchance smite the ball more than once?" With Gallic-shoulders shrug to indicate he was aware of nothing untoward, Henri was silent. Jean, who was everywhere recognized as the game's consummate sportsman, somehow wouldn't bring himself to protest, and Cochet escaped to win three games later his first of two Wimbledon men's singles titles.

I so much wanted to believe Henri wasn't really sure about his double-hit but could never really convince myself. In France, Henri was everyone's "The King." A year later, I became Cochet's practice mate and fractured-French interpreter prior to his winning our U.S. Nationals.

CHAPTER THIRTY THREE

Henri Cochet –
The French Connection

HENRI COCHET, A STEEL SINEWED RARITY OUT OF LYON, France, was the only true magician the game has known. With a serve your grandmother wouldn't trade for, Henri would step up to mid court, and handling his racquet like a toothpick, half-volley your returns.

The most imaginatively memorable shot I have ever borne witness to was at a France vs. U.S. Davis Cup doubles match in Paris. Cochet made a move to poach on an anticipated John Van Ryn crosscourt forehand return of a serve by Cochet's partner Jacques Brugnon. Rather then belting his assured cross-court forehand return, Van Ryn instead belted the ball down the alley. Henri pirouetted 180 degrees clockwise and with back to the net and blind to the ball, made contact for a crazy winner. He was so damned creative he made us all feel we were in chains. Big Bill Tilden, John McEnroe, Frank Sedgman and perhaps Yannick Noah are the only other players I can think of to remind me of a few, but very few, of Henri's electrifying improvisations.

Henri's reasonably hard first serve landed in the box perhaps half the time, but neither first nor second could break a canary egg. However, he was deceptively clever enough to keep those run-around forehanders from cramming the ball down his or his partner's throat. Henri's primary objective: to make his way to the net, where his one-in-a-million powers of anticipation made him ten feet tall!

First-time opponents who might assume, as I once did, that Henri could be a profitable lobbing target, were quickly disabused. He had an uncanny ability to get comfortably under every ball, however deep, and sweet-spot hammer the ball for sharply-angled winners. Let me offer a provocative tidbit how this four-time No. 1 would have fared against such mid-moderns as Pancho Gonzales. It was about five years after Cochet's retirement that Donald Budge rocketed onto the tennis scene. Knowing that from age 15 I had seen most of Henri's big-time matches, as well as twice playing him, Don once asked me if Gonzales wouldn't have made mincemeat of his second serve. You can say I gave Don pause by noting that Frank Shields could garner but a single set of the eleven he played against Henri in major events. It happened that Don's question was posed only minutes after he had barely survived a 6-4 fifth set of a Newport match against inspired but over-the-hill Frank, and Don's legs were aching from crouching down to receive Frank's blockbuster serves.

Cochet spoke barely a word of English when he came to America and captured the U.S. Nationals in 1928, accompanied by a wife, mother-in-law and a mixed doubles partner. My sputtering French persuaded him to invite me to serve as both his interpreter and practice mate. I had played him fairly close at Roland Garros that May (Henri tended to get a bit careless at times), and though I was only 16 at the time and a bit startled by the *menage a trois*, it sure didn't deter me from accepting Henri's hugely flattering invite. France's famous Four Musketeers of tennis, as Henri Cochet, René Lacoste,

Jean Borotra, and Jacques "Toto" Brugnon were known, were ever supportive teammates throughout their decades of widely disparate careers. I frequently ran into Jean, a much-traveled businessman, but René and Henri were somewhat closer pals of mine, and whenever Paris comes to mind, their images loom.

Henri Cochet

CHAPTER THIRTY FOUR

Foot-Faults...
Before and After

SURPRISINGLY, MANY TENNIS-INVOLVED PEOPLE ARE unaware of the dramatic difference that the advances in equipment, weekly competition and rule changes have contributed to the caliber of play of the modern game.

They are amazed when I tell them that our game's 1968 rule revisions have had as much impact on the overall abilities of the modern pro players as the 25 percent to 30 percent "faster" new racquets and near-weekly tournament play. Such amendments as the change-of-side's 90-second rest allowance, versus "play shall be continuous," and bathroom recess and injury time-outs are helpful to the often bone-bruised competitors. But the "home-run" motivated foot-fault rule change has been by far the most beneficial development for today's multiple rocket-launching servers, for both first and second deliveries.

For the first half-century of the rise of tennis as an international major sport, servers were required to keep one foot behind the baseline and one foot in contact with the ground until the ball left their racquets. You now see the game's 140 mph prodigy Andy Roddick hitting the ball with four or so inches of air underfoot and his in-front foot landing three to four feet inside the baseline. The overall advantage? A major forward advance of three to four feet for your first volley, not to mention the increased body leverage that adds to service velocity. This effectively means that the 36-inch height of the center strap becomes perhaps 3/8" lower. This may not sound important, but when you're a paltry 5'10" (as I was), and your serve often contacts the rope-hemmed net-tape, believe me, it's a different ball game.

With our game's armchair critics again protesting that the increasing frequency of aces is killing off the alleged spectator-preferred rallying exchanges, all the regulators need do is re-store the original foot fault code – then encase themselves in their bullet-proof vests, as those now multiple bazooka bom-bardiers vent their collective ire!

CHAPTER THIRTY FIVE

French Frustrations

IT IS CURIOUS TO NOTICE THAT A SURPRISING NUMBER of the sport's all-time greats have the Roland Garros jewel missing from their crown of Grand Slam tournament achievements. The sluggish courts of crushed red brick at the French Championships have been a frustrating obstacle to master for numerous Hall of Famers and have denied many a tennis legend from entering its winner's circle.

For a number of frequently less renowned French winners, the victory has brought them a slice of tennis immortality, though their basically backcourt play has inhibited their chances at any of the other three faster-court majors.

Because the French Championship has been such a thorn in the side of so many four-Slam aspirants, I'd like to expound a bit on why so many top-ranked stars have failed to make the grade. A victory at Roland Garros is of sovereign importance if one is to attain the Olympian summit of tennis of winning all four major titles in a single year – the Grand Slam – a feat only achieved by two men, first by Don Budge in 1938 and again by Rod Laver in 1962 and again in 1969.

For those who might be uncertain why the French is a different ballgame from the other three majors, it should be explained that its playing surface is not what is often mistakenly referred to as "clay" but a fine grit measurably slower-than-its-American-cousin Har-Tru. Roland Garros always played slow, but after a rain shower – Wow!

Multiple major tournament winners thwarted in their quest for the French title include such grass and hard court powerhouses as John Newcombe, Bobby Riggs, Jimmy Connors, John McEnroe, Boris Becker, Stefan Edberg, Pete Sampras and Patrick Rafter; and though I may possibly end up at risk with certain of my peers, I am impelled to hazard these comments as to why certain other high-echelon strivers failed to bring home *le jambon*.

Connors had marvelously flat and accurate ground strokes, so strong on "normal" surfaces, but at Roland Garros they would lose their zip. Could he have compromised by rolling a few and hanging in there with occasional volleying sallies? Becker fired nothing but howitzers in France, where everyone gets an extra step to reach their salvos. McEnroe had nearly all it took, but the slow stuff doused much of his first-serve fire and his chip-and-run-in style tended to set him up for passing shots. Edberg and Rafter were both great serve-and-volley whizzes who didn't get quite enough on their deliveries in Paris to force the floater returns they could put away on grass and hard courts. Stefan made it to a final in 1989 but couldn't quite muzzle the passing shots of the extraordinary prodigy Michael Chang. Lastly, and particularly puzzling to me, there's Sampras. Pete's normally devastating serve and forehand lost a lot of clout on the slow-mo French clay. He was never convinced that no matter how exasperating, it was a no-win game unless he could have cut down the pace and worked the rallies until he got one to clobber or go in on. Losing to Andrei Medvedev in the second round in 1999, Sampras said, "On every surface it's natural instinct. Sometimes on clay my instinct is not the right call. Maybe it's best to stay back, maybe it's best to take a little off my serve and come in on the next shot. I get into a hole, and I want to serve my way out of holes. On clay, you just can't do that."

You'll hear it from past champions who've garnered a French victory en-route to other triumphs: until a Grand-Slam event winner hammers out a French win, he hasn't yet earned the privilege of sharing the unique luster of those who have.

CHAPTER THIRTY SIX

Mark McCormack - The Ultimate Sports Mogul

UNCOUNTED FLAGS WERE AT HALF-MAST WHEN MARK McCormack's heart, as stubborn as any that beat, finally gave out after a four-month battle to survive a disastrous cardiac arrest. The 72-year dynamo of vigor and ebullience seemed invulnerable to anything less than ultimately natural causes. Even though the sad ending appeared inevitable, the finality of it was a shock.

As one who is proud to be counted as a decades-long friend, as well as one of Mark's early days' associates, the following revisited vignettes from our 40-year relationship present a side to Mark that not everyone has been privileged to know.

For starters, way back in 1964, I dreamed up the idea of a marquee name, national-franchised laundry and dry cleaning chain, modeled after our Budge-Wood Service success in New York City. The country's leading dry cleaning equipment company was about to introduce a daringly innovative dry cleaning development and had expressed interest in backing my approach. Unquestionably, a charismatic Arnold Palmer title on the door would immensely benefit our marketing concepts, so I phoned Mark who suggested I meet with him at New York's St. Regis hotel. A couple of days later when I knocked on his door, it flung open and this guy points a finger at me, hollering "I saw you beat Frankie Parker in Chicago!" That was my introduction to Mark McCormack.

In his youth, Mark wanted to be a tennis player, but when his father moved the family into a house alongside a golf club fairway, Mark was encouraged to learn that game - and did well enough to qualify for the National Amateur and two majors - yet he retained his yearn for "our" game. I later drove down to Philadelphia to meet Arnie, who was in a tournament at the Whitemarsh Club. Arnie, a Pennsylvanian to the core, ordered a couple of boilermakers. Fairly soon, there was little talk of business but much of golf and tennis and, yes, the deal was done. Next scene was where Mark and his attorney-pal, Bob Burton (whose father had been a Supreme Court Justice), would work with me on our agreement. It may not be easy for those who perceived Mark as a billion-dollar, probably ruthless business tycoon, to picture him breaking into guffaws in the midst of serious negotiations, but that's the way it was with us. At one point I felt the need to get a kink out of my back and lay down for a roll on the carpet, with Mark and Bob immediately following suit. The papers were drawn in no time flat, and I threw an announcement party at my hobby-born Town Tennis Club. As something of a wordplay addict, I suggested a "Suits You To A Tee" logo (with a golf tee image in place of the letters), which Mark sprung for.

At that time, Mark had just three clients, Arnie, Gary Player and Jack Nicklaus, but the near godlike Arnie, once his college golf opponent, was the meat and potatoes on his budding IMG agency plate. With computers not yet even on the drawing board, Mark's personal recording of his stable's activities was written in minuscule script, three names per a single line of his legal pad.

At a breakfast meeting with Mark and Arnie, Arnie told me that after a dozen stops and starts, he had quit smoking for good. Not five minutes later, one of those uniformed "Call For Phillip Morris" singing delivery boys walked in the door to deliver a box of smokes to our table. On the way out, Mark asked me if I thought there was any real cancer threat involved if you didn't inhale. That's how little real knowledge there was at the time about the danger. Mark once sent me a gold cigarette lighter which my son Godfrey much coveted. I told him it was his if he promised to never again light up. He never did and I owe you, Mark!

On the funny Mark side, he once called to tell me he was celebrating a triple-client coup and asked me to guess the identities of three famous people whose names' last syllables were pronounced "e" as in "eek" - I flunked, and he said it was Pele, Killy and Twiggie.

Our joint Palmer franchise venture was a near-immediate winner, with over a hundred outlets opened over the first two years, but as Arnie's winning ways began to fade so did our franchise applications. Eventually, in what was to become recognized as a typical Mark McCormack business brilliancy, Arnie's basic operating business activities, including ours, were sold to NBC, or a subsidiary, and my share of yearly royalties was properly appreciated. Every couple of years, I'd receive another of Mark's four best-seller business books. He somehow stole the hours to record his diverse experiences.

Any number of would-be imitators have tried but failed to come within miles of imitating Mark's winning formula; but his leapfrog growth was a very personal reflection of an innate honesty and understanding of the alchemy of relationships. The names of especially famous people who've entrusted their reputations and financial futures to IMG is fairly common knowledge, but to accent the near-unimaginable variety of Mark's clientele let me name-drop a past or present handful of these legendary special people: Arnie, Nicklaus, Tiger Woods, Michael Jordan, Rod Laver, Pete Sampras, the Williams sisters, Derek Jeter, John Madden, Jeff Gordon, Joe Montana – and are you ready for this? General Electric's Jack Welch, Pope John Paul II, Margaret Thatcher and the Smithsonian Institute. As a measure of Mark's relationship with many of his clients, Monica Seles is his son's godmother.

One of the last times I saw him at Wimbledon, I dropped in on him holding court at luncheon in his hospitality tent. He rose from his chair and literally lifted me off my feet while introducing me as the guy who'd sold Arnie to innumerable American housewives. After a few catch-up exchanges, one, his telling me he'd recovered enough from an earlier setback to start playing some tennis again, he then asked what he could do for me, or me for him. I said I thought I had something cooking that might warrant becoming an IMG client, and he held out his hand, announcing to his dozen or so guests that he needed another "Woods" on his roster. He then told me that among non-stop other moves, he'd ventured into the Asian TV soccer market to become the world's third largest TV company with over a thousand on his London staff. Wow!

A mildly rephrased offering of the poet W.H. Auden proclaims, "I like a good number of people, but the only ones I can love are those who make me laugh." That you sure could, Mark, and thanks for the memories.

CHAPTER THIRTY SEVEN

Adrenaline

NOWADAYS, WHENEVER A TENNIS PLAYER PUMPS ONE'S fist after hitting an exceptional shot or blasts an ace to save a break point, the TV boys or girls often talk about adrenaline. They're on the right track but miles from the finish line.

I can speak as one of the surprisingly few athletes I've found to have experienced the extraordinary effect of a full scale "adrenaline attack." Because of my own three-time occurrences with what I must characterize as a phenomenon, I questioned a number of friends as to whether they had undergone anything like this, and only four – Rocky Marciano and Archie Moore, the world-famous boxers, Johnny Weissmuller, the Olympic swimmer turned Tarzan, and Babe Didrickson, the standout female golfer, track and basketball star who could arguably be the greatest-ever athlete, boy or girl – could positively identify the symptoms. When the chips are really down, the winning tennis guys count on adrenaline for an important up-tick in their execution percentages, but none I questioned recognized anything like what I described as happening to me. As a pertinent aside, of all the greats of tennis, Pancho Gonzales has to have been the best-ever chips-down server. Jack Kramer, a legend himself, told me that his tally of Pancho's break-against first-serve efficiency over a 100 pro-tour match span showed a jump from his average of 56 percent first serves to an unheard of 87 percent!

My first encounter with this esoteric adrenaline visitation was when I was 18 and playing Wimbledon runner-up Wilmer Allison in Southampton's Meadow Club final in 1930. I was down two sets to one, love-four and love-40 on my serve. Precisely at that point, a sort of electric surge welled up in

Sidney Wood strikes a forehand

me. I had goose bumps all over and my hair felt as if it were standing up. My first reaction was that I might pass out on the court, and I headed for a linesman's chair, flushed with emotion and about to burst into tears. Almost immediately, I wiped my eyes, threw off the towels, pushed away my concerned sympathizers and bolted for the baseline.

Here it gets even crazier. I served three clean aces and two unreturnable balls. I was too young to have any idea what all this might mean, but I must have played almost perfect ball to mount an insurmountable eleven-game winning streak.

The initial, wildly emotional reactions slowly abated, but a strange remoteness descended on me. The crowd seemed far off and my concentration was trance-like and dead calm. Everything seemed to focus on the brilliant emerald area, inscribed by the white boundary lines. My clarity of vision seemed to magnify the size and fuzziness of the ball and its speed seemed to slow up. My reflexes, coordination and absolute certainty of anticipating every shot was beyond anything I had felt before. I knew the ball would find the center of my racquet and obey my commands. I still have no idea how long such adrenaline occurrences will sustain themselves, but however brief, they are sobering experiences.

The second time for me was in a Davis Cup match at Wimbledon in 1934 against the Aussie great Jack Crawford, then the world's No. 1, who the previous year was one set shy of becoming the first player to win a Grand Slam after losing a five-set final to Fred Perry at the U.S. Nationals. I won the first two sets when the rains came and put us over for the next day. Sounds great continuing with such a lead? Forget it. A front-runner knows that he may not carry his winning form into the next day, also that any top-level opponent who's behind invariably plays tougher.

The following morning, Jack couldn't miss and suddenly I'd dropped two 6-4 sets and we were even up – except that I was also down love-two and love-forty on my serve and about to blow America's whole Davis Cup year. Then again, that unreal, giddy feeling enveloped me, and this time I had at least some inkling of what might occur. With aces seemingly on call and my game under its errorless, hypnotic influence, I reeled off six virtually uncontested games for perhaps the most critical win of my career. That win over Jack, coupled with Frank Shields' subsequent 6-4, 6-2, 6-4 win over Viv McGrath capped our U.S. team's comeback from 0-2 down against the Aussie team – the first and only time to date that a U.S. Davis Cup team has come back from the brink to win a best-of-five match series.

Fifteen years later I was playing Bobby Riggs in another Meadow Club final on a brutally hot and humid day. It was something like four-all in the fifth set when I began to feel a little dizzy and I plopped into a linesman's chair. At that late date in my competitive life, it never occurred to me that this could be another adrenaline thing. In fact, a spectator-doctor advised it was sunstroke and ordered me to default. By dinner time, I felt like a million bucks, suffering only from the possibility that my misdiagnosed sunstroke might have been another long-absent adrenaline visit, and I might have taken my third Meadow Club title and, with it, the club's legendary player-inscribed bow trophy.

In between these years, I once or twice attempted to induce an adrenaline reaction by dramatizing my plight in relatively important matches. Although it wouldn't take, I've wondered whether it might be possible to train one's mind to produce such a result. I had neither the background nor the time to research the idea but my experiences have kept me more than mildly curious. For instance, could the supreme heroics of Alvin York, the heroic World War I figure, and Audie Murphy, the most decorated American soldier of World War II, and other unsung acts of selfless bravery have occurred without some inspirational stimulant? There are the mind-hobbling exploits of Harry Houdini. Could they have been accomplished merely by illusion, coupled with fantastic dexterity and the respiratory control needed to remain submerged past known physiological limits? Or could this remarkable man have schooled his extraordinary mind and body to stir his emotions on cue into a trance that would provide him with the powers required to perform these feats?

I have no idea why, from among an apparently limited number of others, I should be invested with the occasional capacity to release this latent attribute. It's enough just to count my scattered blessings.

A few years ago, I was vividly reminded of my episodes by a National Geographic TV sequence showing a rhinoceros being strangled by a boa constrictor. The snake was several times coiled around its victim, who was on his feet trying to shake the creature loose. After a desperate series of futile attempts, the rhino toppled to the ground, presumably lost. But in only a few seconds, with tire coils visibly tightening, the rhino erupted into a galvanic convulsion, and, lo, the strangler was shaken from one of its encirclements then thrown completely free. With a few shakes of his head, its near-victim simply trotted off. This extraordinary manifestation of the forces of self-preservation that lie dormant within us stirred me profoundly.

• CHAPTER THIRTY EIGHT •

Analyzing the Greatest Players of All Time

BILL TILDEN VS. PETE SAMPRAS OR ANDRE AGASSI? GIVEN today's immensely more power-packed racquets, who would pick up the marbles? And how about Rod Laver, Don Budge, Fred Perry, Jack Kramer, Pancho Gonzales, René Lacoste, Henri Cochet, Jean Borotra, Ellsworth Vines, Bobby Riggs, Lew Hoad, Tony Trabert, Frank Sedgman, Ken Rosewall, Arthur Ashe, Jimmy Connors, Bjorn Borg, John McEnroe, Boris Becker, Ivan Lendl or Stefan Edberg?

Such questions are constantly put to every player whose repute and venerable status give credence to one's observations, and even present-day tournament players and chroniclers of the game have an abiding interest in the player-comparison opinions of those they consider eminently qualified.

In fact, at an International Tennis Hall of Fame dinner at Newport a few years ago, Bud Collins, the globe-trotting tennis sophisticate, who was aware that I'd qualified for my first Wimbledon at the unlikely age of 15 in 1927, surprised me with the Tilden-contra-the-world question. He told me the sport of tennis was in need of a book by someone who had seen all the great matches and played "everyone" and that I was also the only guy still around who could first-hand compare and record what every tennis buff would hope to know.

Computers now spit out weekly rankings of over 1,000 players on a weekly basis, but back when punch cards were its high-tech breadwinners, national amateur rankings were determined by committees appointed by each country's tennis association (no more than fifty players were ever rated in the United States) and rankings of the world's top 10 were decided by a succession of self-appointed London sports columnists whose judgments sometimes appeared based as much on favoritism as fact. Add to this the fact that from 1930, when "Big Bill" Tilden departed the amateur ranks, until 1968, when Jack Kramer led the pro contingent into the "Promised Land of Open Tennis," the pros were barred from all major tournaments and excluded from the world rankings. This rendered the rankings meaningless as a measurement of the world's best. Also prior to 1968, virtually every newly-anointed amateur champion would be lured to the pay-for-play game, thereby stripping the amateur ranks of its marquee drawing cards and permitting as yet unproven contestants to be crowned No. 1 in the world of "officially-sanctioned" tennis.

The effect of this double standard? Just tote up the number of stadium-filling superstars lost to the major amateur events through the schism: Tilden in 1931, Cochet in 1933, Vines in 1934, Perry in 1937, Budge in 1939, Riggs in 1941, Kramer in 1948 (following the five-year World War II gap) and, during the next two decades, Gonzales, Sedgman, Hoad, Rosewall, Trabert and Laver all bid adieu to the trophy-only circuit.

With each season's cumulatively diminished quality of competition, the paths to Grand Slam glories were measurably eased for the succeeding year's hopeful. Put another way, with Wimbledon as our focus, Tilden would have been the bettors' favorite to garner another two wins; Budge, at least another four or five; Riggs, Kramer and Gonzales, three to five each. As for Trabert, Hoad, Rosewall and Laver, who knows how many among them? Pre-1968 winners such as Wood (ouch, that's me!), Ted Schroeder, Yvon Petra, Vic Seixas, Jaroslav Drobny, Bob Falkenburg, Budge Patty, Dick Savitt, Ashley Cooper, Alex Olmedo, Neale Fraser, Chuck McKinley, Roy Emerson and Manolo Santana all would have been hard-pressed to squeeze out even an occasional win against their abdicated amateur opponents.

Three all-important extenuations bear on the records of our brightest of stars and we must comment on their merits in order that the reader may interpret their relative importance, vis-a-vis the overall picture of the half century under review.

For example, the first U.S. airborne wayfarers to Wimbledon and Paris were in 1946. Before that time, the boat trip to Europe was a five-day affair plus the absolutely essential need of a week to find your land legs. Each year you could safely predict that half the top seeds who would debark from the boat from Wimbledon to the United States to compete, usually the next day, in the Meadow Club tournament, and would be out of the singles after the first or second round, would be left to quench their frustrations on the sunny Atlantic sands of Southampton. All in all, it took about eight weeks to make the scene at both Paris and Wimbledon, while from Australia, this period was more than doubled. Often the trip was economically or otherwise unfeasible for the reasonably-pure amateur of those days.

The second consideration was the advent of World War II, which resulted in a six-year championship hiatus from 1940 to 1946 at Wimbledon, Paris and Australia; and, with most of the players in the service, there was a low-level entry at Forest

Hills. In virtually every sport, leading athletes lost out on the opportunity to enhance their records during their prime competitive years. In tennis, this especially affected players such as Don Budge, Bobby Riggs and Jack Kramer.

The final consideration has to be the development of pro-tour tennis, which lured the leading performers to its ranks and prevented their participation in the four major events and Davis Cup. Until 1968, these men were precluded from defending their Wimbledon, Forest Hills and other crowns by the simon-pure rules in effect.

When Rod Laver went pro in 1963, he was fresh off winning his first Grand Slam, in which he dominated and beat everyone in the amateur kingdom. But, here again, there was quite a way to go before he would become a case-hardened touring pro. Though there were to be no more head-to-head professional barnstorming matches, Rod met Gonzales in meaningful tournament matches over a two-year span but could win only a few. How would he have fared after more seasoning and the years had cooled some of Pancho's fire, we'll never know.

Also until 1968, Davis Cup regulations prohibited professionals from competing for their countries and over the previous ten years, during which there was high-purse pro tennis decimating the upper reaches of the amateur lists, the world's best were not participating. This is sad for such a long-recognized important goodwill-builder among nations to be only a minor factor in the considerations of the player's individual world ranking.

A fair question would be to ask where I get the gall to take on this project. At the age of 14, and almost 90 pounds, I won the Arizona men's singles, which earned me entry to that year's U.S. Nationals, the modern-day US Open. The following spring, I was shipped to Paris for the French Championships and shockingly won two rounds to become the youngest-ever male qualifier for Wimbledon. There, I played defending champion René Lacoste on the hallowed Centre Court on opening day. In 1931, I became the youngest-ever Wimbledon men's singles champion at the age of 19 (Boris Becker broke my record in 1985 when he won the title at the age of 17). From that time on, through to the late 1970s (doubles only towards the end!), I was privileged to compete against virtually every top player in the world. At the start of the organized pro game, I invented and patented the cushioned, transportable Supreme Court, which is still used for indoor events, and I was not displeased to be reminded by an old ATP buddy that there was no way the pro indoor circuit could have gone full bore had I not dreamt up the concept.

It is these years of experience and fraternal relationships that permit me to confidently assess the pecking order and relative aptitudes of my tennis brethren in our star-studded galaxy from nearly the dawn of competitive tennis, my aim being not to determine who belongs in any year's top 10, but how the best would stack up against the best, in any year, past or present.

I'm positively no misogynist, so why would I not have included all those richly deserving ladies in this discussion? I have been present, or have viewed on TV, virtually all important women's matches going back to the Helen Wills (Moody) era, and I do indeed have opinions as to which stars of the gentler gender belong on which rungs of the all-time ladder of tennis greatness. However, it would not only be more appropriate, but a better qualified assessment if such an analysis were undertaken by one of their own leading ladies who has shared the competitive scene.

My rankings are based essentially on win/loss records in important events, primarily the four majors – the Grand Slams - and the pre-1968, head-to-head pro tours, with appropriate credits accorded Davis Cup competition and other important events. What lies behind the printed scores is what determines the placement of each of the world's great players. For instance, for many years certain tournaments have traditionally counted more than others. After 1946, when the top-amateur-turns-pro system resumed, the purely pro events such as the U.S. Pro Championships, Wembley, and the WCT Finals in Dallas became important. Finally, judgments have to be made of the relative value that should be attached to such factors as longevity, consistency, two-man tour results and the ability to win on the slow as well as the fast surfaces.

THE TOP FIFTEEN

1. Don Budge: A no-brainer. In 1938, Don was the first winner of the Grand Slam and for six decades he has been recognized by his peers as the one player to have commanded not only every shot in the book for every surface, but also to have been blessed with the single most destructive tennis weapon ever—a bludgeon backhand struck with a sixteen ounce "Paul Bunyan" bat. All opposed? You might first want to check out Jack Kramer's required reading, *The Game.* Jake knows all, tells all. Wrote Kramer in the book, published in 1979, "Don is still the best player I ever saw, and (Ellsworth) Vines is next. Right away a lot of people are going to say I'm an old timer, pushing the guys of my era. Don't I know that the human body runs faster and jumps higher now than in the 1930s? And I say, yes, I know that, and will you please name me a better hitter than Ted Williams and a better singer than Caruso?... I feel fairly confident in saying that Budge was the best of all. He owned the most perfect set of mechanics and he was the most consistent...Day in and day out, Budge played at the highest level. He was the best."

2. *Jack Kramer:* The choice is clear to me, but may be less so to certain of today's forty to fifty-year-olds; but even a scan of Jake's professional stats tells you why he was a rung above Pancho Gonzales (who in turn handled all the rest).

3. *Bill Tilden:* Most sports fans know Bobby Riggs (thanks in part to Billie Jean King, who beat him in the famed 1973 "Battle of the Sexes" match), René Lacoste and Fred Perry (their shirt labels!), but poor Henri Cochet, Jean Borotra, Pancho Segura—even Budge, Kramer and Gonzales!—are becoming shadowier with time and better remembered by historically disposed fans. But everyone has heard of William T. Tilden. In his day, Big Bill was as world famous as Jack Dempsey, Bobby Jones—even Babe Ruth! He changed the game's image from a side-court chair, standing-room sport to a stadium-packed, crowd-pleaser (it was Bill who paid the freight on America's first tennis stadium at Forest Hills). The press named his pile-driver first serve "The Cannonball" and, allowing for the transformation of tennis racquets, no one other than Frank Shields and Ellsworth Vines ever owned one better. Bill's enduring record on every surface—an absolute master of every shot in the book—make him a shoo-in for third on my list. Were there more witnesses around who'd seen Tilden

play everyone in sight until the age of 48, I might well be sued for leaving him off the top. In spite of his constantly troubled lifestyle, Bill, together with his mighty contemporaries, Jones and Ruth, must go in the books as a once-in-a-century sports aberration.

4. *Pancho Gonzales:* Other than for his nemesis Kramer, Pancho dominated the pro touring field after leaving the amateur ranks after winning the 1949 U.S. Championships. He had many one-sided win records against such Grand Slam event champions-turned-pro as Frank Sedgman, Tony Trabert and Ken Rosewall.

5. *Rod Laver:* He won the first of his double Grand Slams as an amateur in 1962, but in his 1969 win he had every active pro in the game to vanquish. His only significant tournament disappointment was his failure to win a WCT title, losing two finals to an inspired Ken Rosewall (their second match in 1972 was one of the greatest I've ever seen). There will understandably be many who can't comprehend why I place a two-time Grand Slam titleholder midway among the first ten, but in my opinion, when comparing Laver's strokes to these other great champions, this is the position in which I feel he belongs.

6. *Pete Sampras:* You know all about those weeks without end as numero uno, his multiple Slam record, especially his virtual ownership of Wimbledon's Centre Court. His understandably respectful peers were resigned to playing second fiddle to Pete, but they looked forward to ambushing him on slow clay. But it is Pete's inability to capture a single French Championship - perhaps to equate with Ivan Lendl's frustrating naughts at

Wimbledon - that puts a hold on marking him ahead of other unbeatables who've done it.

7. *Fred Perry:* Where do you put a player who practically waltzed through three straight Wimbledons and two of our national singles, plus an Australian and French for sweeteners? This, of course, is Fred Perry who did his winning when all the big guns except Vines were around to test him. After he turned pro, Fred played a 61-match neck-and-neck tour with Vines, 1936-37 (Vines won, 32-29), but he began to sag a bit thereafter (Vines beat him head-to-head 49-35 in 1937-38). Barnstorming was not this Britisher's cup of tea, but he belongs at no less than number seven among the splendid ones.

8. *Bjorn Borg:* Bjorn practically toyed with everybody through an astounding six French Open wins, but none of us sage old timers gave him a chance to make it past the second round on Wimbledon's fast grass. Yet overnight, our high-roller, back-court habitue became a demon volleyer and for five consecutive years, he made mincemeat out of such grass-court winners as Ilie Nastase, Jimmy Connors and John McEnroe. Borg stood an impossible four to five feet behind the baseline to take first serves, but was so fast out of the blocks that few wide slices got past him. He was one hell of an athlete. Could he have continued his dominance on the hard courts of the US Open, Borg would have been a shoo-in to be ranked ahead of all others, but on the hard courts of Flushing Meadows, his second delivery lacked the weight to defend against McEnroe's chip-and run-in tactics, and Bjorn had to settle for a runner-up role.

9. *Ivan Lendl:* To me, Ivan was an enigma wrapped in a Centre Court frustration. He'd gladly have refunded Wimbledon's

first prize guineas several times over for just one win, but his best chance was in 1987, when he lost to the lower-ranked Pat Cash. Lendl beat all comers hollow on everything but grass, so why couldn't he make it? Unlike Borg, no matter how many hours he ultimately spent striving to become a volleyer, habit was too strong. On crucial points, he couldn't bring himself to leave the baseline and rush to the net, where Bjorn never feared to tread. Nonetheless, with three US Open titles, three French Open titles and two Australian Open titles and an astonishing 11 runner-up showings at majors (totaling 19 Grand Slam tournament finals), how can he not rate an upper berth-spot.

10. Jimmy Connors: Jimmy won eight major singles titles and was an eight-time runner-up. He failed to win only in France where he was unable to capitalize on his flat-hitting power. I was among those who urged Jimmy to stop feeling he had to bury every ball from the baseline, but it wasn't until his waning years in the big time that the light finally dawned. In his later years, he was a born-again net rusher, but think how many of those lost finals he could have converted to victories had he unshackled his game and groundstroke fixation a decade earlier.

11. John McEnroe: McEnroe's most remarkable season was 1984. He lost just 13 games in two final-round, straight-set wins in major finals over Connors (Wimbledon) and Lendl (US Open). That's incredible. At the French, he had Lendl nailed but admitted he blew it and lost after leading two-sets-to-love. If the TV could have been programmed to cut out all but John's shots in play, you would have been admiring perhaps the most naturally gifted shot-maker ever to play tennis. McEnroe's great record of three Wimbledon and four U.S. titles, plus four major runner-up showings, puts him high on our ladder, but with even a modicum of self discipline (and regard for our game's image), I'd bet he could have traded his odorous court garbage for more than just a few more wins.

12. *Boris Becker:* I've had a personal interest in Boris and his career ever since 1985 when he cleaned Kevin Curren's clock to take the first of his three Wimbledon titles while erasing my 54-year span of being its youngest winner. Boris had a serve with an affinity for the Centre Court turf. He can give you a heavy whack with both his first or second, or slice it with wicked deception. He won one U.S. singles title and two in Australia, but Roland Garros refused to succumb to his power game.

13. *Roy Emerson:* When Roy wound up on his serve, he looked as if he were bowing to Wimbledon's Royal Box, which could be habit-formed from having accepted the winner's trophy there successively in 1964 and 1965. Elsewhere he walked off with two U.S., two French and a mere six Australian singles titles. Although these were before the Open era of tennis (1968), don't knock it. Roy had what it takes.

14. *Stefan Edberg:* Stefan is almost a throwback to bygone years when the big events were on grass and 80 percent of the game's best were serve-and-volleyers. Edberg's was not a big serve, but his sure-handed, superbly-reflexed and fearless net play won him two titles at Wimbledon, the US Open and the Australian Open, plus a runner-up showing at the French in 1989. How many more would be crowding his trophy

room if he could have waltzed in behind such trenchant deliveries as McEnroe's, Becker's, Ivanisevic's, Sampras's and Krajicek's? Double maybe?

15. René Lacoste: Inventor of the first ball-throwing machine, the metal racquet and, of course, the chemise Lacoste, René had a tennis game that was every bit as mechanical as his creative brain. As the leader of the Four Musketeers of the courts (with Henri Cochet, Jean Borotra and Jacques Brugnon), René combined his Maginot Line defense game with pinpoint angled, counter-attacking ripostes. His two Wimbledon, two U.S. and three French wins were against such toughies as Bill Tilden and his compatriots Cochet and Borotra.

You might notice that there are some major omissions from this list of top 15 players of all time. Of course missing are the greatest players of the current era, Roger Federer and Rafael Nadal, as well as Andre Agassi, a winner of eight majors, including a career Grand Slam. My father was fortunate to have the opportunity late in his life to watch these three compete, but was not able to put his thoughts down on paper as part of this compilation. However, he was a big fan of all three players and would no doubt have place them in at least the top 10 of this list.

Of Federer, he said he was the most intelligent player he had seen in over 50 years. Of course winning more major singles titles than any other man would place him near the top of this list. Unfortunately, my father passed away just months before Federer won the 2009 French Open that completed his career Grand Slam, and his record-breaking 15th major singles title weeks later at Wimbledon.

In addition to admiring Nadal's ferocious physical game, my father admired Nadal's great sportsmanship. My father came from an era in which sportsmanship was expected and the rule of the day. Nadal's char-

acter and how he presents himself was not lost on him. While my father was not around to see Nadal clinch his career Grand Slam at the 2010 US Open, that milestone achievement would have rated him very high on this list.

Agassi was a player who grew on my father. When he first burst on the scene, my father detested his long hair and look – preferring the clean-cut style of his own era. In fact, he would often go out of his way to not watch Agassi play. Through the years, however, he began to appreciate him more and admired his strength, speed and the way he played and took great joy in watching him in action. If Agassi's final body of work (established after my father's writing) is considered, he too would rank well against the players mentioned in this list, especially with his eight majors that included at least one each of the Big Four.

- David Wood

CHAPTER THIRTY NINE

The Greatest Strokes and Skill-Sets of All Time

Throughout his life, my father had a fascination with comparing the games and shots of the greatest players from all different eras. This was born out of being so frequently asked how the players of yesterday would stack up against the stars of the present. For many years, he was the last surviving player of his generation and the only living person who had personally seen all the greats from Bill Tilden and the Four French Musketeers through Pete Sampras and Andre Agassi.

His following commentary provides an excellent view of my father's perspectives and opinions of the greatest shotmakers and skill-sets in the history of the sport. This compilation was written – and added onto – in the 1990s to the early 2000s, so readers should not be alarmed that certain stars of today are missing. However, we felt it important to publish these writings to document for posterity his observations of men's tennis through the span of his life.

- David Wood

THROUGH THE DECADES, ONLY A HANDFUL OF EXTRAOR-dinary shotmakers have stood head and shoulders above their peers in executing a certain one of the essential strokes of tennis. What I have attempted to document is a history of the sport's master hitters in all categories of play. Not all these players mentioned have won major titles, but each has simply executed his special prizewinning shot better than all but a favored few since the game began.

The current generation of players are harder hitters in every category except volleying, where, of course, it's control that counts, not ball-speed. So with no direct or otherwise reasonable means of comparing a wood racquet-user's skills to those of today's better-equipped performers, I am delighted to submit the following. Verily, if the top two or three players in each of the last five decades were permitted a year or two to take advantage of the bigger and better new racquet and to become proficient in the now essential top-spin backhand (and the extra step allowed by the modern foot-fault rule), all would make it to the upper rungs of present-day ladders. Granted, there would be a zillion more tough hombres to beat out, but the intangibles that make time-proven winners in any way do not melt away.

In terms of physiques, today's inches taller, stronger, pasta-pampered champions indeed have a decided advantage over those of yesteryear. However, unlike basketball and football, height and heft don't count as much in tennis. Such sub-six-foot shrimps as Bobby Riggs, Rod Laver, Ken Rosewall, Lew Hoad, John McEnroe, Jimmy Connors, Andre Agassi and Michael Chang—as well as other former world No. 1s Carlos Moya and Marcelo Rios—have not fared too poorly. (And while on the long and short of it, there's football's little old Doug Flutie, who, after winning the Heisman Trophy with Boston College, fared quite well in the National Football League and in the Canadian Football League as well, earning CFL MVP honors.)

Although only marginally-applicable to my theme, I cannot resist adding that for a truly objective selection of any all-time greatest, the accomplishments of his predecessors must be given due consideration. In this regard, I offer a sampling of ever-magic names and numbers to conjure with. Babe Ruth's 60 home runs – and the 61 of Roger Maris – in baseball (and who will equal Ted Williams's and Ty Cobb's plus-400 batting averages?); Paavo Nurmi's 4:10 mile time went untouched for eight years and 14 more passed before Roger Bannister overcame the four-minute-mile brainwash block. Add to this the unforgettable Jesse Owens, Hitler's Olympic anathema, who took four history-making sprints in all of four days.

I sometimes sense that today's crop of young tennis touring millionaires have the idea that the game really began only a dozen or so years ago – that the Tildens, Budges, Perrys and Kramers were great names for the plaques on the walls, but would have been pretty helpless if they reappeared on the scene today and tried to compete in the "new game." Most of the action movie clips of the "good ole days" have the players darting around like Max Sennett dervishes and are more amusing than impressive. But I have news for you, boys. Both Ellsworth Vines and Frank Shields, for instance, loved to blow an average of two clean aces past you per game. That's the hard-to-believe rate Vines maintained over the course of the 39 tour matches he played against Don Budge in 1939. Try giving that handicap away to a couple of guys who could also power their forehands past you-at-net just as often as the players of today.

And that's only a sampler. I haven't seen many new groundstrokes in the "new game" that would have out-stunned the forehands of Vines, Shields, Bill Johnston, Bill Tilden, Fred Perry, Jake Kramer or Pancho Segura or the backhands of Don

Budge, René Lacoste, Jack Kramer or Bobby Riggs.

As the opening gun of every point in every game, the serve must be rated at about double the importance of any other shot in tennis. My full analysis is of not only the basic shots, but of other satellite strokes and attributes, and who executed each the best, from my eye.

THE SERVE

On June 23, 1991, *The New York Times* gave special mention to Goran Ivanisevic uncorking ten aces against Pete Sampras to win the pre-Wimbledon tournament in Manchester, England 6-4, 6-4. This means he served 10 times and averaged an ace a game—roughly Pete Sampras's own average for his semis and finals wins at the 1990 US Open.

Aces are to tennis what homers are to baseball, three pointers to hoopsters and KOs to fight fans. Which big-time servers over the years have owned the most feared deliveries? Most are familiar with the exploits of the super servers of recent years, but a glance at the headliners of prior decades affords an interesting overview of the big guns of our game who have made the crowds roar.

Let's start with those all-time most notable ace makers: Ellsworth Vines, Frank Shields, Gottfried von Cramm, Bill Tiden, Lew Hoad, Don Budge, Goran Ivanisevic, Pete Sampras and Andy Roddick. Which of them should be numero uno is a toss-up, but from my view, these players stand above all others. An ace per game service average is mighty good stuff, but would you believe two-and-a-half? That's about what Vines and Shields could consistently deliver, and without the double-fault equalizers that seem to plague many of the current power servers.

In 1939, Vines, with howitzer hits that could shock a seismograph, averaged 2.36 untouchable serves for each service game of a 39-match pro tour head-to-head against the Grand Slam-winning colossus Don Budge. To boot, almost a third of these contests were played on clay!

Vines' aces, however, were not only against Budge. In his first Wimbledon final against Britain's Bunny Austin in 1932, he blew Bunny apart 6-2, 6-1, 6-3, searing Centre Court with 30 clean aces. His form was the model for both Budge and Kramer, but neither could quite match his power and accuracy. Elly's first serve was clocked at 122 mph, slightly faster than the serves of Shields and Lester Stoefen, a fine U.S. Davis Cupper in my day. Measured against today's 130-140 mph higher readings, this doesn't sound like much, but bear in mind that "in those days" they measured the speed as the ball crossed the net, a 39-foot distance to decelerate. Today's readings are taken from 18 to 24 inches after the ball leaves the racquet. It should also be noted that today's numbers are also bolstered by modern day racquets that produce 30-40 percent more power.

Allison Danzig of *The New York Times*, the great tennis writer of his era, reported Shields as delivering 2.4 aces every game commencing with the quarterfinals of eight successive grass court tournaments during the summer of 1931. In the obituary I wrote about Frank, I told of his once hitting a 24" x 24" service box target plate in a 100-ball, Davis Cup exhibition an unimaginable 56 times in succession. He was hitting them dead flat at about 85 percent speed all this with an old-time wooden bat, connecting with the target a total of 67 times over all. George Lott, Johnny Van Ryn and I hit a combined total of 37 out of an allotted 300! I've never since heard of anyone making more than six bull's eyes in a row. Remember DiMaggio's 56-game hitting streak? *Ripley's Believe It or Not!* featured both his and Frank's never-since-approached numbers. Years later, in seeking to test the ball-skid speed of an Astroturf surface, I enlisted the hard-serving American Davis Cupper Barry MacKay into trying the same 100-ball target test. However, he missed so many that I finally gave up. I couldn't wait to tell him about Shields!

Just a mite below Vines and Shields, in a tier of "second echelon" servers, are Bill Tilden and Don Budge. I would rank them a short step ahead of a sizeable group of elite bombers, our third echelon, whose roster includes, in chronological order; John Doeg, Wilmer Allison, David Jones, Lester Stoefen, Gottfried von Cramm, Jack Kramer, Bobby Riggs, Bob Falkenburg, Pancho Gonzales, Jaroslav Drobny, Lew Hoad, Stan Smith, John Newcombe, Arthur Ashe, Roscoe Tanner, John McEnroe, Ivan Lendl, Boris Becker, Pete Sampras, Goran Ivanisevic and Andy Roddick.

For sheer shot-making drama, no one comes close to Tilden, and the press titled his flat serve "The Cannonball." Its speed was a shade below 112 mph, but his short, rapid windup gave him the deception needed to power in more aces than any before him. In a memorable sequence against René Lacoste in the 1927 U.S. Finals, Bill was down love-40 and match point, but banged in three clean aces and two unplayable serves to win the game. That he ultimately lost the match is forgotten, but the overlapping roars of the Forest Hills stadium crowd were remembered for years.

Budge's other weapons, particularly his fearsome backhand, caused people to overlook the potency of his serve. Don would blast about an ace and a half a game with his 16 ounce blunderbuss racquet. Until he injured his shoulder in an army training session, he made everyone feel like a middleweight in the ring with a super heavyweight. Don's great serve and backhand were the weapons that won him all four major titles in 1938 – the "Grand Slam" – a feat shared only in men's tennis by Rod Laver.

In rough chronological sequence, here are those we have named as our third echelon's best ever.

John Doeg had only a prayerful push for ground strokes but, backed by a failsafe volley, his Gatling gun first serve made him a standout. A big lefty who took his stance a yard off center, he could slam a flat one down any line or, with the same frictionless motion, throw a huge slice at you. In his final-round match at the 1930 U.S. Championships against Shields (he had upset Tilden in the semifinals, while Shields had taken me out) and serving to the left court, Johnny actually curled two slices into the marquee box seats. And the term "double fault," a familiar call to McEnroe, Becker and too many of the modern serve crunchers, was not even in his vocabulary.

I can tell you from a very personal experience that Wilmer Allison had one heck of a first serve. When we met in the finals of the 1935 U.S. Championships at Forest Hills, I raced off to a 3-love, love-40 lead when, to my distress, Wilmer blew three clean aces by me, added two un-takeables and went on to clean my clock. Allison and another American player Berkeley Bell were the only two players who served with both feet together and toeing the baseline, but the pivot gave them all the power they needed. As evidence that great athletes will ever beat convention, look at McEnroe's equally weird service stance.

Stoefen was my occasional doubles partner. The cannonading "Stoef" had a classic service motion which became the pose

model for most tennis statu-
ette prizes and promotional
placards. His serve was so
picture-perfect that his windup was used as the original
Association of Tennis Professionals (ATP) logo! The 6'5"
Stoef hit a great first ball, but
he was not always consistent.
In fact, we had the great doubles team of Allison and Van
Ryn on the ropes in the semis
of the National Doubles with
a lead of two sets, a service break and 40-love on Stoef's serve.
After missing each of the next three first balls, for reasons only
he could tell you, he decided to go for an ace on the second.
He again missed all three and we ended up blowing the game,
our momentum and the match. If we'd been playing for prize
money, I'd have killed him, but instead, we both just roared
with laughter at this crazy performance.

Gottfried von Cramm had the ill fortune to make the big
time in an era that spawned such titans as Don Budge and Fred
Perry. He won two French singles titles but lost in three successive Wimbledon finals (two to Perry and one to Budge) and
again to Budge in memorable five-set matches in Davis Cup
and the U.S. Final. His first serve was worth an ace-per-game,
but what we remember most of our German Baron friend was
his high-rise, wicked twist second ball.

Although no challenge to Vines and Shields, David Jones's
serve is worth the telling. He hit his first ball flat and heavy,
but if it missed, he'd add another 10 percent to the pace, and,

apart from aces, his second delivery was one no one ever tried to move in on. Being a college basketball star, Dave may have reasoned that when you miss the first freebie, you go to school on the range and seldom miss the second basket. Dave never won a major, but, strictly on his Big Bertha serve, he upset Cochet at Wimbledon and Vines at Newport.

Bobby Riggs was not generally thought of as a top-rank server but believe me his was as tough as all but a few. Because of Bobby's flawless motion and coordination, his 5'9" height in no way reduced his acing ability. His deception and changes of pace forced you into a lot of foul tips which Bobby unfailingly pounced on for put-away volleys.

Early in his career Jack Kramer found that he could win more points by taking ten percent off his flat serve and going for accuracy and deception. You could rarely get set for a solid return off his serve and Jack's percentage on first serves must have been close to 70 percent. He would follow his first and second with trenchant, sure-handed volleys, and his technique made him the winningest of all touring pros during which he humbled prematurely pro-enrolled Gonzales and made a believer of Riggs. Jack's success influenced a generation of would-be stars to play it his way, rather than go for the outright ace.

That Bob Falkenburg won a major title with groundstrokes your grandmother wouldn't trade for is a distinction which the 6'5" 1948 Wimbledon men's singles champion shares with Doeg and 1949 Wimbledon champion Ted Schroeder. The feat is comparable to a fighter going into a championship bout with a broken right hand. Bobby's was the only serve I've ever seen that you couldn't read whether it would slice wide or jump to your backhand until it hit the ground. His nitro-packed delivery would surely have registered in the 140 mph count – on par with the best of the modern players.

If any one player proved the point that a real star had to have something under the hood to accelerate, it was Pancho Gonzales, who survived more break points than anyone before or since. Jack Kramer kept track of the first serves that Pancho slammed in on game point-against over an entire year and told me his average was an impossible 87 percent. This compares to what was probably 50 percent when no crisis impended. It was not easy to love the churlish Gonzales, but you had to hand it to him for the gritty attributes that made him the "King of the Hill" for over a decade against the redoubtable likes of Hoad, Rosewall, Trabert, Sedgman and Segura.

Lew Hoad could bang in his first serve with the best, but what made him such a feared opponent was the way he covered the net on every return. The Australian once administered a forty-minute rout of Gonzales in a national pro final which prompted Don Budge to say that this was the greatest tennis exhibition he'd ever seen. What is sometimes forgotten is that Lew was one match from winning the Grand Slam in 1956, losing to Rosewall in the final of the U.S. Championships.

Jaroslav Drobny was a cunning lefty powerhouse, one of the few pre-war Europeans to develop a proper serve motion. It carried the native Czech to a Wimbledon title in 1954 and French titles in 1951 and 1952.

When I first saw the tall, blond and handsome Stan Smith at the Los Angeles Tennis Club, I remarked to Perry Jones, the "Dean of Tennis" in Southern California back in the day, that Stan looked a little too stiff to make it big. Was I ever wrong! Stan matched John Newcombe ace for ace in their memorable Wimbledon final in 1971, which was a close encounter of the slugging kind. His serve carried him to the Wimbledon title in

1972, after winning the U.S. title the previous year.

John Newcombe could serve an ace a game, which, added to his big second ball and a fine forehand, took him to the winner's circle at Wimbledon in 1967, 1970 and 1971, Forest Hills in 1967 and 1973 and the Australian Open in 1973 and 1975.

Arthur Ashe had one of the best backhands ever and was an extraordinary tactician, but it was largely his many aces that won the critical points needed to bring home the bacon. He won the first U.S. title that was open to pros and amateurs in 1968 and also took home an Australian title in 1970 and Wimbledon in 1975.

You wonder how John McEnroe could unwind from his weird stance, but when he did, he hit a load of outright winners. His slice to the backhand court was his big breadwinner. His serve and volleying carried him to three Wimbledon titles, four US Open titles and earned him recognition as one of the best doubles players ever.

Ivan Lendl had a big serve, but a noticeable flaw was his high toss, which affected consistency in outdoor play. Stadium winds will gust and swirl, and when the ball doesn't come straight down to your racquet, there goes your groove. Why didn't he throw it lower? Just try changing your own toss after years of doing it the same way. Never!

In the last quarter century or so, Boris Becker had one of the fastest of serves that on some days made him almost unbeatable. If his volley was a bit more dependable, Boris would have been even tougher. Pete Sampras had a natural swing, big serve and well-rounded, strong supporting shots that have led most of the "we've seen 'em all" players to tab him as the greatest of all-time. Goran Ivanisevic had a beauty of a flat serve – and wicked lefty slice serve – but didn't have the temperament to be consistent. Ion Tiriac once picked him to win five Wimbledons, but alas, he won only one in 2001. Andy Roddick fired an ace at a Davis Cup match in 2004 that registered 155 mph on the radar gun. Wow!

A fair question might be why so many former power guys did better than current top ten players, particularly since modern racquets add more than 30 percent to the ball speed and revised foot-fault rules let your feet leave the ground and either foot cross the line. A partial answer could be that the modern balls are slightly slower than before, but the best answer must simply be "anomalies." Every sport has them.

And what about the second serve? With today's 30-plus percent more powerful bats and dipping backhands, you need a bigger second ball to cut the chances of getting zapped on your way to the net. A swerving slice to the forehand, a high-rise twist, some small deception and positively no fadeouts at break point would also be required.

Take your own count of the biggest acers of modern times – Sampras, Ivanisevic, Roddick, Richard Krajicek, Mark Philippoussis, Greg Rusedski and others and you'll see precious few whamming as many as one and a half per game over a full match then start matching up the double faults. Granted that today's second serves must be more potent, thus riskier, to offset the composition racquet-wielder's tougher returns, it does leave one wondering whether Vines and Shields might have been disbarred had they been around when those elbow-saving slingshots hit the circuit.

What might be accomplished by some super server who'd grooved his delivery to serve aces on two out of three attempts, and to shoot for the ace on every second ball as well? It doesn't require a computer to establish that anyone who could count on a two-thirds success ratio on every serve could scarcely do worse than earn a tiebreaker every set he played. Perhaps a basketball player's experience with "freebie" shooting might prove instructive for our mythical ace server. As you may have observed, when a shooter misses his first free throw, the minor adjustments he makes for the second measurably enhance his chances of sinking it. Might there not be a similar opportunity for the tennis server? David Jones was the only player I knew of who went all out on his second serve. In a Wimbledon quarterfinal, he aced me three times on his first and five times on his second. Food for thought?

For some realistic input on this theme, I sought out Lou Carnesecca, the famed coach of the St. John's University basketball team, who advised that the second basket would be some 40 percent likelier to drop. Are you ready to go for it, you 140-mph guys? The only hitch is that our hero could bomb out with four straight double faults to lose the game; but even if he followed with eight straight aces to maintain his two-thirds average, he'd still be a break down. Oh well, let someone else worry about that.

Proceeding from fantasy to reality, I continue to hope that some less convention-bound tennis striver will eventually take time off to test the potential for such a concept. One day, some seven-footer with six-foot coordination may come along and give it a try. Then they'll have to change the rules or perfect a four-foot racquet to level the playing field.

FOREHAND

There are many more varieties of the forehand than meet the casual eye. There is the spectator-recognized power stroke of players like "Little Bill" Johnston, "Big Bill" Tilden, Fred Perry or Ellsworth Vines from the 1920s and 1930s or from players like Jim Courier, Pete Sampras and Andre Agassi from more modern times. This shot is designed to back up the opponent or win the point outright. There is the more subtle, sharply-angled forehand that was best demonstrated by players like the Ecuadorian Hall of Famer Pancho Segura, Fred Perry and Henri Cochet. This is a shot that makes your opponent scramble wide. Then there's the on-the-rise short swing, punched shot that carried players like Cochet, 1950 French and Wimbledon champion Budge Patty, Lew Hoad and John McEnroe up to the net countless times against an opponent's serve. Ivan Lendl and Courier were the best of the modern-day sluggers.

BACKHAND

Jimmy Connors – and later Andre Agassi – belted two-handed backhands without abandon. Borg, with a two-handed backhand, along with Ilie Nastase and Guillermo Vilas with one-handed backhands, influenced many to adopt the topspin backhand as a superior defense against the net-rusher as well as a wear-em-down baseliner. No one could club a one-handed backhand like Don Budge, but Kenny Rosewall's drives were also smooth and deadly.

SERVE AND VOLLEY

Jack Kramer is most known for this style of play and I place him, Lew Hoad, Rod Laver and John McEnroe as the best of all time in this category. They were the ones who best developed a combination of the two shots. They could throw in plenty of first-serve aces, but their fundamental strategy was to save these big hits for when they were in a hole and go with the better percentage game of winning points with two or three shots instead of one.

Kramer could throw in plenty of first serves but saved the big hits for when he was in a hole. How did it work for him? Boy did it work!

OVERHEAD

There are two reasons for not hitting an overhead in the air. The first is because the wind is making it tough to hit. The second is that a lob is extra high and the ball is picking up speed every foot it drops, and is tougher to catch just right. There have been a few players who actually preferred to let all but the very deep lobs hit the ground first. The best at this was Berkeley Bell, who would position himself like a trained seal under a rubber ball, and, sometimes on his knees, Bell would blast the hovering sphere for a put away. Bell reasoned, and not incorrectly for his torso-control aptitude, that in this way he would be able to pinpoint the ball on the sweet spot of his racquet more surely than he could expect if he had to deal with its rapid acceleration in descent. Lew Hoad, Pete Sampras and Jack Kramer were also no slouches when it came to belting the overhead.

FOREHAND VOLLEY

The above-waist forehand volleys differ from the lower-height ones in that many players hit the former with a short forehand drive swing. This is because the relatively high returns coming at you are slower (or else they're heading out) making it feasible to swing a little on the shot. Almost all the Europeans swing on their high forehand volleys to get the pace they need on their slower clay surfaces. John Newcombe and Lew Hoad also took a pretty good cut at it. The true "purists" such as Budge Patty, Jean Borotra and Berkeley Bell have depended more on taking the ball further in front of them and putting more snap into it.

A below-waist forehand volley is basically a punch. The only freak hitters were Borotra and my former Davis Cup teammate Wilmer Allison, who gambled – and mostly made out – on outright placements for the first hit. Allison seldom bothered to go to your backhand. He was so wired into his crosscourt that he could slam it out of reach time after time. Naturally, this close-margin hitting resulted in a few bad upsets when his timing was off, but on good days this weapon carried him to major-event wins over Cochet and Perry in their primes.

As for the best volleyers, I would give the nod to Pete Sampras, who performed most of his serve-and-volleying tactics on the grass while winning seven Wimbledon titles, along with Allison and Patty.

BACKHAND VOLLEY

Props for the best backhand volley span many different generations, starting with Henri Cochet from the 1920s, Don Budge from the 1930s, Rex Hartwig from the 1950s, Ken Rosewall, whose career spanned the 1950s to the 1970s, John McEnroe, who graced the courts in the late 1970s through the 1980s, and Stefan Edberg, who served-and-volleyed from the mid-1980s through the mid-1990s.

The above-waist backhand volley is the one that brings forth the "oohs" and "aahs" from the grandstand. There have been relatively few spectacular hitters of this basic, but hard-to-perfect stroke. Most of the standouts have unique styles. Borotra, for instance, used to hit his with his elbow actually above the racquet head. Don't ever try it his way if you don't want a tennis elbow for a lifetime playmate. Tony Trabert used an almost "western grip" so that the racquet face was angled downward. He could hit the "wrong way" to your forehand without even thinking where his feet were. Jimmy Connors used two hands to belt his. And Don Budge? No use trying to explain any type of backhand he ever hit. Don handled that 16 ½ ounce bat as if it were a hairbrush – and he could part the sidelines with it!

The guys who executed the below-the-waist backhand volley the best are the ones who got their feet where they belonged so they could jab the ball down your forehand line or slash it to your left side with equal assurance. As distinguished from their forehand counterpart, all the best low backhanders (except for the unreal Borotra) put plenty of slice on their shots and rarely missed one. Frank Sedgman had a beaut, with Rosewall and Ted Schroeder just a shade less potent.

HALF-VOLLEY

Of all tennis strokes, this is the most difficult for most players to master, in my opinion placing such gifted artists as Henri Cochet, Rod Laver, John McEnroe and Frank Sedgman as the best ever. To play the half-volley really well calls for a special kind of reflex and the ability to coordinate footwork and body balance to accommodate the vagaries of wind, spins and bounce differentials. Most of the great half-volleyers seem to be more born than made. Cochet, Sedgman, Laver, and McEnroe looked as if they could do it just as well with their eyes shut. Ken Rosewall came by his shot out of sheer necessity, as practically every able serve returner could clobber Kenny's weak offerings to his feet. Cochet's serve was even less powerful than Rosewall's but, as those privileged to have seen this little wizard in his heyday could also attest, Henri could have handled these normally tough chances standing on his head.

DROP VOLLEY

Although closely akin to the backcourt drop shot, the drop volley, while calling for as sure a touch, requires less disguise. This is, of course, because of the shorter distance it travels from the net position and because the victim has less time to see it coming. Many more drop shot opportunities present themselves at net than from the backcourt, and players who best mastered the shot, like Bill Tilden, John McEnroe, Ilie Nastase and Pancho Gonzales, won countless quick points by chipping their volleys close to the barrier rather than going for pace and depth.

For most players, the backhand drop volley is easier to disguise than on the forehand, simply because it is executed with the same downward, easy high-to-low motion as the full forehand volley. It's a beautifully deceptively simple-looking shot to observe when "feathered" over the net by the hands of such consummate masters as Gonzales, Nastase and Laver.

DEFENSIVE VOLLEY

The special requirements of this shot are, basically, exceptional reflexes, the shortest of backswings and plenty of controlling bite on the ball. The best of the defensive volleyers are usually among the best of the doubles players, for it is here that safety, and not force, at net pays dividends. You could hammer the ball all day at a player like George Lott, my former Davis Cup teammate, the Aussie great John Bromwich, Don Budge's doubles partner Gene Mako and the doubles-excelling Musketeer Jacques Brugnon and it would get you nowhere. In singles, there's too much court to protect and the sure but soft volleyer gives away too many chances to a strong groundstroker.

ANGLED PASSING SHOTS

Here the over-spin is more important so as to pull the ball down more quickly. Rod Laver, he of the amazing, one-of-a-kind wrist flicks, was also among the best in this category and it worked wonders for him. He could turn the ball into a leaden egg with his amazing wrist flick. Bjorn Borg put almost as much roll on his shorties and was deadly accurate even when scrambling – and was deceptive as well. Bobby Riggs and René Lacoste from yesteryear counted on deception and pinpoint sharpshooting.

THE DROP SHOT

In the hands of the soft-touch artist, the drop shot can pull an opponent's cork. The secret is disguise and control. When refined to the science that, for instance, Bill Tilden, Bobby Riggs, Pancho Segura and John McEnroe distilled through the years, it can wreak havoc with a baseline player's game plan. Without a flicker of an eye, or discernible alteration in the swing, the real artists can switch from the expected attacking shot to their well-veiled undercut dink. Best attempted off a well-placed, moderate-height return and taken on the rise, the drop shot looks rather simple to execute, but don't you believe it.

Although a majority of players hit their normally sliced, shorter-swing backhands with more deceptive drop-shot results than they can achieve on their forehands, players such as

Riggs, Berkeley Bell and the Japanese standout Jiro Satoh, who occasionally sliced, or even chopped, their forehand ground strokes, were past masters at fooling you with a well-undercut forehand angled chip. And it was Segura who, with the threat of a big on-the-rise hit, together with his short, two-handed swing, could quickly "bite" the ball short before you could even gather yourself for a sprint.

REFLEXES

All top players have excellent reflexes. However, those we have selected for this attribute are the ones who would make most of us look almost sluggish by comparison. In Henri Cochet's biographical sketch, we describe an impossible shot that he pulled off at net, while fellow Musketeer Jean Borotra would slingshot across the forecourt as if he had a firing pan under each foot. I have seen Frank Sedgman, Gene Mako and, of course, Cochet casually await a big overhead and routinely pick it off their shoelaces.

ON-THE-RISE SHOTS

While theoretically an on-the-rise ball should be easier handled when the racquet is also moving upward, in practice, the Lavers, Rosewalls and McEnroes have had such precise timing that they have hit most of these shots with a slight undercut. Don Budge met his dead flat, while Lew Hoad, Tony Trabert and Don McNeill, the 1939 French champion and 1940 U.S. champion, mostly rolled theirs. A chancy shot for most people, the ones who have perfected it can't wait to gobble up any ball that's short enough to make a move to the net more feasible.

Equally dramatic to watch has been that mere handful of athletes whose exceptional coordination has enabled them to attack deep returns from a few inches off the ground just as confidently as most of us do off a normal high bounce. Budge never seemed to care at what height he caught the ball—his feet and his body always seemed to be perfectly positioned. Then there's the picture of Fred Perry streaking along the baseline and picking the ball off the ground with his wristy continental forehand as if he were handling a table tennis ball (ping-pong to you). It happens that Fred also won a world championship at that game. We should not depart from this shot without mentioning that the greatest backcourt half-volley slugger of all time was R. Norris "Dick" Williams, who won two of our Nationals and played some unconscious sets with a wicked return of serve with practically no balls getting more than 18 inches off the ground. Dick's active career ended a couple of years too early to be included in our ratings list but, as non-playing captain of our 1935 Davis Cup team, I played lots of doubles as his appreciative partner and we came out no worse than even in Davis Cup practice against such redoubtable teams as Lott-Van Ryn and Budge-Mako.

LOBS

Often maligned by those who don't either understand its effectiveness or simply can't get the knack of this easy shot, the lob is as essential to tennis play as any stroke in the book – and this applies to singles and, almost as importantly, to doubles.

The offensive, normally top-spin lob, as contrived so deceptively, for example, by Don McNeill, Bjorn Borg, Ilie Nastase and Guillermo Vilas, is a weapon that has dampened the ardor of countless net-rushers. Nothing is more devastating than to be caught in the act of crouching down to await the anticipated, tape-level passing shot, then helplessly watching the parabola arching out of reasonable reach before you can uncoil to spring upward.

A sure-handed defensive lob, too, has turned many an important match around. In the final of the 1963 U.S. Championships at Forest Hills (the modern-day US Open), I saw that fine tactician Rafael Osuna go to work on one of the game's big lob-killers, Frank Froehling, Jr. With strictly defensive lobbing and agile retrieving, Osuna broke up not only Froehling's vaunted overhead, but as so often happens, his confidence in the rest of his attack.

RETURN OF SERVE

It's my view that seventy-five percent of first serves and ninety percent of second serves are directed to the backhand. Therefore, the forehand return doesn't sound so important. But the term "directed to" is misleading. The more agile, better anticipators will often manage to jump on a sliced or a spun first delivery – the usual means of getting to the net – and the persistent run-around forehand slammers, such as Pancho Segura, Bill Johnston and Bill Tilden, were able to cut away into that ninety percent second-serve figure. Moreover, the threat of this maneuver will force many servers out of their normal patterns and reduce their effectiveness. Andre Agassi and Jimmy Connors could also belt with the best of them.

FIGHTING SPIRIT

This factor is such a prerequisite to championship performance that it is impossible to cite ten champions, out of all the others who have played the game, who have not possessed it. However, we want to add our interpretation of fighting spirit to round out our collection of descriptions. Every enduring champion in every sport possesses an inner reservoir of fight to convert the irretrievably lost contest into victory. Fighting spirit is part ego blended with fear of humiliation, part animal instinct laced with the loosely-used term "adrenaline," intelligence that allows the competitor to correctly gauge an opponent's condition and state of mind, to calculate a risk, and to act upon a signal when it's time to switch tactics. But, most of all, fighting spirit is the gift of absolute form at the moment of crisis – concentration that can marshal one's strength and coordination and steel the nerves to burn in an ace or thread a passing shot through a six-inch opening.

THE FINISHING TOUCH

Because everyone else on the circuit has every bit as much fighting spirit, per se, as all great champions have, the inexplicable inability of the others to get that last winning point over the net is worth commenting on. Over the years, there have always been certain near-the-top players who, for reasons that have escaped the understanding of their loyal fans, seem to find a way to lose important contests. Because they were such really great strokemakers – particularly outstanding are Lester Stoefen, Frank Kovacs and, surprisingly, Japan's two greatest stars, Jiro Satoh and Jiro Yamagishi – it is hard to understand why they never became champions. The first time that I went up against any one of them, I could see no way that my lesser equipment would let me win. But as each match progressed, some competitive instinct would tell me that, if I could hang on long enough, something would give. Except for the one time Satoh put me out in the Wimbledon quarterfinals, it worked that way. Even in that match, Jiro let me pull even from 1-5 in the fifth set.

TACTICS/GENERALSHIP

Here's where we separate the men from the mentalists. The vast majority of players spend long hours in vain pursuit of unattainable perfection. Everybody is out there practicing the bang-bang serve-and-volley and harder and harder groundstrokes they hope will enable them to hang one on the likes of Bjorn Borg, Jimmy Connors or John McEnroe. It's a rarity that we see a player's game vary from match to match no matter how many times one may have failed to beat his man with it before. The Borgs and Connorses and McEnroes of the modern era, and the Lavers, Kramers and Budges before them, had so much firepower that they seldom were called upon to do more than reload the bullets. Borg, however, found that to turn the tide against Connors' early advantage in victories, he must try something new. He surprised us all, and perhaps even himself, by cutting down the roll on his shots and by becoming a successful net-rusher in the 1978 Wimbledon final.

When we think of master strategists and tacticians of the game, the first names that clear the tape are Bill Tilden and Bobby Riggs. Both had every kind of slice, twist, loop, lob, dink and drop shot, plus that inborn sense of how to ad lib a shift of tactics to keep an opponent from being comfortable no matter how far they were ahead.

Another surprisingly successful tactician was Arthur Ashe, who detected weaknesses in Connors' short game and parlayed it to a stunning victory at Wimbledon in 1975. I saw Arthur also pull the plug on Guillermo Vilas at his peak with similar "soft-balling" in the final of the old Barry McKay Cow Palace event in San Francisco.

Before the 1978 Wimbledon final, I cabled Jimmy Connors a reminder of his above-average volleying skills and of his earlier Grand Prix win against Borg in which he took nine of 13 points with some well-spaced serve-and-volley ventures and an occasional change of pace. But although these tactics had worked for him, the lesson inexplicably failed to register, and my cable, if received, fell on deaf ears as Jimmy stayed in the backcourt. This was to be Connors' third loss in the Wimbledon finals (followed by his fourth in 1984) and I turned off the televised match in exasperation at this palpable waste of what every tennis player cherishes as golden opportunity.

All kinds of moves constitute "tactics." Here's one that has worked for me. The long respected and seldom violated maxim "Never change a winning game" is another of those dangerous generalities. As a basketball fan, I've watched and wondered in the company of millions at the almost frittering away of "insurmountable" leads.

Basically the same thing occurs in tennis, but not nearly so frequently. Among all top competitors, the toughest job is to maintain a hot streak while comfortably ahead or to keep control over a first-class opponent who has been performing below par. The term "outclassed" doesn't apply in high echelon competition. In most contests, it is only a hair that divides the winner from loser and the guys that are behind can be counted on to come back strong from a poor shooting spell. Seasoned athletes do not fold. With less to lose, they get looser and tougher, while the ones ahead know from long experience that it is psychologically next to impossible to sustain a high percentage performance after piling up a big lead.

As a born iconoclast, I came to recognize this truth at an early stage in my own career and have had reasonable success in thwarting my opponents' comeback efforts before they could turn things around. Naturally it didn't always work, but my method was to sometimes change tactics at a point in the match that I judged my adversary had about worked himself out of his starting slump and adjusted to whatever kind of shotmaking had gotten me ahead. The decision to switch from a winning game is kind of like deciding what is the highest ticker-tape price hold-out for taking a profit on a rising stock.

In the next NBA game you watch, when some team jumps to a twenty-point lead, think what moves you, if you were coach, might make to hold on to that margin.

SLUGGING

It is easy to observe which players are slamming the ball – not so easy to know who is able to do it day in and day out and on the clutch points. Of the ten heavy hitters we have named, all but Bill Johnston, Elly Vines and Jack Kramer slugged off both wings; and only Johnston and Jack Crawford fail to qualify as big servers. Dick Savitt, Tony Trabert and Jack Crawford seemed to hit what the players call a "heavy" ball rather than strictly a fastball.

When Don Budge and this writer were discussing Crawford's shots, Don asked me if I didn't think Jack's shots were heavy. I said I did and I asked Don to define "heavy" for me. Neither of us could truly say what made balls feel heavy, except that when Crawford hit them they came over like a 16-pound shot. As for sheer ball speed, both Johnston and Vines occasionally blasted forehand passing shots at me from the baseline that actually cleared my racquet before I could bring its head up.

CHAPTER FORTY

Friendships for a Lifetime

THOSE OF US WHO HAVE BEEN PRIVILEGED TO BE A PART of the upper echelons of international tennis competition have, in time, happily succumbed to the special bonds of friendship that are born out of appreciation of one another's struggles to achieve. The intense and often bitter rivalries of earlier days sooner or later mellow and dissolve into less passionate, often humorous memories. They are replaced by an inherent mutual respect for one another's talents as well as an understanding of all the years of dedication, humbling frustrations and moments of exaltation that are the rungs on the ladders to stardom.

When you've been head-to-head with a man for five cliff-hanging sets, well past the point of reasonable exhaustion, you get to read him well – his thinking, strategems, self control, conceits, humor, grit and basic fairness under fire. It is a more intimate confrontation than you'll develop from trading amenities at a cocktail party.

To a large degree, the same camaraderie prevails among athletes in other sports. Stan Smith told me once after competing in the televised series "The Superstars," where athletes from a variety of sports competed against each other, that all the contestants felt they had known one another all their lives. Virtually all athletes consume every line of the sport pages, and each feels he really knows the other athletes he reads about. In essence, those who have made the big headlines have shared much the same experiences in reaching their goals.

Of course, there is the occasional misanthrope who can't shed his ego enough to forgive and forget or welcome the more enduring rewards of friendship. But during my 20 years or so of upper-level match play, all but a handful of my opponents of every nationality have become much cherished cronies.

When I made my debut at Wimbledon (on Centre Court no less) at the unlikely age of 15, it was against the former champion René Lacoste. Lacoste, whose crocodile shirt you probably now wear and whose metal racquet invention sparked a boom in that area, was reasonably gentle with me and we remained friends for many years. During the tournament, I was the interpreter of some curious language between René and Taki Harada, the great Japanese player of that era. When I visited Tokyo in 1971, Taki, whom I hadn't seen in four decades, threw a sake party for me with every Japanese player who could walk being present. Some may not have walked since!

When my wife and I visited the Lacostes in Paris later in life, René gave a surprise lunch for us, and almost every past and present ranking French player showed up. When the welcoming speeches began, I was affected beyond articulation.

H. W. "Bunny" Austin, England's great Davis Cup competitor and nemesis of most United States challengers (me too), for whom I had conceived no undying devotion, crossed my path— literally—in Reno, Nevada 15 years after I'd last played or seen him. From two blocks, unbelieving, we started toward each other and embraced amidst a flood of crazy memories.

The incomparable Fred Perry, who also was not necessarily near and dear to me during those intensely competitive years (it was mutual), much later took me on as a fellow TV commentator and covered me, like the chum he had become, through some sticky, inexperienced moments.

Another vignette from the past recalls Ellsworth Vines, a California cannon. At age 17, Elly and I trained on the courts behind the wooden fences of the Pasadena YMCA. When he exploded onto the Eastern scene with spectacular tournament victories, he also ran short of trousers for the finals (longs in

Fred Perry with Sidney Wood

175

those days). Though inches short, mine had to do. Elly quit tennis for golf way before his time and I didn't see him for years until Wimbledon in 1977. He came up to me and, dead-pan, said "Hello Wood, you got a pair of pants I can wear tomorrow for the presentation?"

On a trip to Hamburg in 1974, a message from Gottfried von Cramm was at our hotel. The "tennis telegraph" must have told him I was coming. Alas, he had left before I arrived and I was not to see him before he was killed in a car crash in Egypt in 1976.

If the premise of kinship through competition ever needed confirmation, it was dramatically there for all to view in 1977 when about 50 former Wimbledon singles champions, men and women, once again made their way from all compass points to the Centre Court to receive medallions commemorating Wimbledon's centenary and to take part in an unforgettably moving ceremony.

I had phoned Don Budge hoping to arrange a flight over with him. Jack Kramer, Tony Trabert and Dick Savitt had also called, but Don said he just couldn't make it. Next scene—Don appeared in the nick of time for the presentations and stood like the colossus he had been astride the Centre Court.

As we lined up, all hands linked, on the greenest of all turfs, with the strains of "Auld Lang Syne" resounding in our ears through the cheering crescendoes of spectators risen from their seats, the memories paraded past my mind's eye, and a hundred hard-fought victories and defeats fused into a single, glowing experience. All that really mattered was being a part of this matchless cohort of ageless fellow athletes who, with rare exception, would be fast friends for life.

Epilogue

I WOULD BE REMISS IF I DID NOT MENTION WHAT I CONSIDER to be my father's greatest achievement, which occurred at the age of 93. From the beginning, my father's life was always full and busy in tennis, business and social activities, as well as with family matters. A life-long workaholic, especially in later years, he never allowed himself any time for anything "extracurricular," least of all religion, which was always the furthest thing from his consciousness. As he advanced into nonagenarian range, he became more and more conscious of his mortality and began to show an interest in learning about God and what the Bible says about our eternity. My older brother, Colin, and I, both Christians, provided him with Bibles and other reading material to aid him in exploring this realm. In 2004, at the age of 93, he made the decision to submit his life to Christ, an astonishing occurrence when taking into account the unusually long, ultra-secular road down which his life took him.

- *David Wood*

Index

Also From New Chapter Press

The Education of a Tennis Player
—BY ROD LAVER AND BUD COLLINS

Rod Laver's first-hand account of his historic 1969 Grand Slam sweep of all four major tennis titles is documented in this memoir, written by Laver along with co-author and tennis personality Bud Collins. The book details his childhood, early career and his most important matches. The four-time Wimbledon champion and the only player in tennis history to win two Grand Slams also sprinkles in tips and lessons on how players of all levels can improve their games. Originally published in 1971, *The Education of a Tennis Player* was updated in 2009 on the 40th anniversary of his historic second Grand Slam with new content, including the story of his recovery from a near-fatal stroke in 1998.

The Bud Collins History of Tennis—BY BUD COLLINS

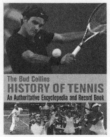

Compiled by the most famous tennis journalist and historian in the world, this book is the ultimate compilation of historical tennis information, including year-by-year recaps of every tennis season, biographical sketches of every major tennis personality, as well as stats, records, and championship rolls for all the major events. The author's personal relationships with major tennis stars offer insights into the world of professional tennis found nowhere else.

On This Day In Tennis History—BY RANDY WALKER

Fun and fact-filled, this compilation offers anniversaries, summaries, and anecdotes of events from the world of tennis for every day in the calendar year. Presented in a day-by-day format, the entries into this mini-encyclopedia include major tournament victory dates, summaries of the greatest matches ever played, trivia, and statistics as well as little-known and quirky happenings. Easy to use and packed with fascinating details, this compendium is the perfect companion for tennis and general sports fans alike.

www.NewChapterMedia.com